W9-BRZ-870

Chicago Public Library

REFERENCE

Form 178 rev. 11-00

The Middle East

Volume 1
BAHRAIN • CYPRUS • EGYPT

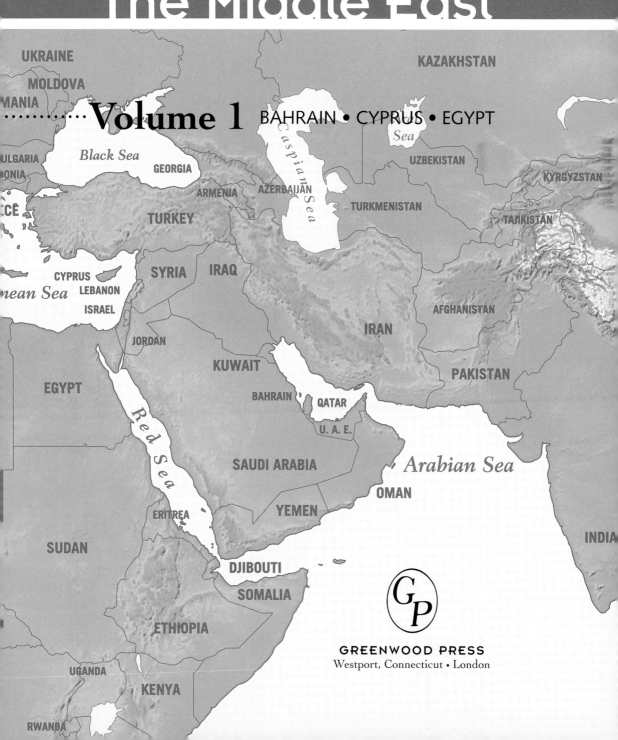

Discovering
World Cultures

The Middle East

Volume 1 · BAHRAIN · CYPRUS · EGYPT

GREENWOOD PRESS
Westport, Connecticut · London

Library of Congress Cataloging-in-Publication Data

Discovering world cultures: the Middle East / by Creative Media Applications.
      p. cm.—(Middle school reference)
      Contents: v. 1. Bahrain, Cyprus, Egypt—v. 2. Iran, Iraq, Israel—v. 3. Jordan, Kuwait, Lebanon,
Oman—v. 4. Qatar, Saudi Arabia, Syria—v. 5. Turkey, United Arab Emirates, Yemen.
      Includes bibliographical references and index.
      ISBN 0–313–32922–2 (set: alk. paper)—ISBN 0–313–32923–0 (v. 1: alk.paper)—
      ISBN 0–313–32924–9 (v. 2: alk. paper)—ISBN 0–313–32925–7 (v. 3: alk. paper)—
      ISBN 0–313–32926–5 (v. 4: alk. paper)—ISBN 0–313–32927–3 (v. 5: alk. paper)
          1. Ethnology—Middle East. 2. Middle East—Social life and customs. I. Creative Media Applications.
          II. Series.
      GN635.N42D57   2004
      306.'0956—dc22   2003044263

British Library Cataloguing in Publication Data is available.

Library of Congress Catalog Card Number: 2003044263
ISBN: 0–313–32922–2 (set)
      0–313–32923–0 (vol. 1)
      0–313–32924–9 (vol. 2)
      0–313–32925–7 (vol. 3)
      0–313–32926–5 (vol. 4)
      0–313–32927–3 (vol. 5)

First published in 2004

Greenwood Press, 88 Post Road West, Westport, CT 06881
An imprint of Greenwood Publishing Group, Inc.
www.greenwood.com

Printed in the United States of America

The paper used in this book complies with the Permanent Paper Standard
issued by the National Information Standards Organization (Z39.48–1984).

10   9   8   7   6   5   4   3   2   1

A Creative Media Applications, Inc. Production
WRITER: Sandy Pobst
DESIGN AND PRODUCTION: Alan Barnett, Inc.
EDITOR: Susan Madoff
COPYEDITOR: Laurie Lieb
PROOFREADER: Betty Pessagno
INDEXER: Nara Wood
ASSOCIATED PRESS PHOTO RESEARCHER: Yvette Reyes
CONSULTANT: Abraham Marcus is Associate Professor of Middle Eastern History and
      former Director of the Center for Middle Eastern Studies at the University of Texas at Austin.

PHOTO CREDITS:
AP/Wide World Photographs pages: x, 2, 8, 10, 11, 16, 30, 31, 34, 37, 47, 49, 50, 51, 54, 57, 58, 60, 62, 67, 74, 78, 84, 85,
      86, 94, 96, 99, 100, 102, 104, 106, 108, 111, 112
© Philip Game pages: 4, 6
© Hulton Archives/Getty Images pages: 12, 14, 38, 40, 43, 45, 76, 90, 95
© Khaled El Fiqi/EPA /Landov page: 18, 23
© Adam Woolfitt/CORBIS page: 21
© Arthur Thevenart/CORBIS page: 26
© Jonathan Blair/CORBIS pages: 33, 52, 69
© Royalty-Free/CORBIS page: 64
© Hans Georg Roth/CORBIS page: 70
© Bettmann/CORBIS pages: 88, 114
© Hulton-Deutsch Collection/CORBIS page: 92

Table of Contents

INTRODUCTION

The Middle East. The name conjures up many different images for most Westerners: fascinating ancient civilizations, the rise and fall of powerful empires, and—most recently—bloody conflicts and suicide bombers. This series introduces the history, customs, and cultures of the people living in the Middle East in the hope of inspiring a fuller understanding of a complex region.

What Is the Middle East?

"The Middle East" is a rather vague name for such an important region of the world. What is it in the middle of? And how is it different from the Near East and the Far East?

Most of the geographical terms used in the world today, such as the label "Middle East," originated with Europeans and Americans. As Europeans explored the world around them, they first headed east. The lands that bordered the eastern basin of the Mediterranean Sea— Anatolia (Turkey), Syria, Palestine, and Egypt, as well as their immediate neighbors—became known as the "Near East." Countries farther away, such as China and Indonesia, were referred to as the "Far East."

The term "Middle East" has been in use for only the past century. It was first used by an American military officer to describe the geopolitical

MEASURING TIME

Most of the world today uses the Gregorian calendar, which is based on the solar year. Because it is a Christian calendar, historical dates have traditionally been designated as occurring before the birth of Christ (B.C.) or after the birth of Christ (A.D., an acronym for the Latin phrase *Anno Domini,* meaning "in the year of the Lord"). In recent years, historians have started to use neutral, nonreligious terms to describe these divisions of time. The *Discovering World Cultures: The Middle East* series follows this practice, using B.C.E. (before the Common Era) rather than B.C. and C.E. (Common Era) in place of A.D. (Some people define the terms as "Before the Christian Era" and "Christian Era.") The dating system remains the same: 1000 B.C. is the same as 1000 B.C.E., while 2003 C.E. is the same as A.D. 2003.

region that included the countries between the Mediterranean Sea and India—those countries in the middle of the Eastern Hemisphere that shared a common culture. Today, there are many different definitions of the Middle East. Some scholars include the countries of northern Africa in their definition of the Middle East. Others use a cultural definition that includes all the predominantly Islamic countries in Africa and Asia. This series adopts the definition used by most modern scholars, adding Egypt to the original list of Middle Eastern countries because of its shared history and Arabic culture.

Birthplace of World Religions

As home to the world's earliest civilizations, the Middle East is also the birthplace of three of the world's major religions: Judaism, Christianity, and Islam. Followers of these three religions worship the same god and share a common early history. Today, about 2 billion people worldwide identify themselves as Christian, while about 1.3 billion follow Islam. Nearly 14 million are Jews. Together, these three groups make up 53 percent of the world's population.

Judaism

Judaism is the oldest of the three religions, originating nearly 4,000 years ago in the land of Israel (also known as Palestine). Jews believe that Abraham, who was born in Ur in present-day Iraq, was the founder of Judaism. About 1800 B.C.E., he began to teach that the world was created by a single god. God made a covenant, or agreement, with Abraham: if Abraham left his home and followed God's commandments, God would bless Abraham with children and establish a great nation. Moses, a descendant of Abraham's son Isaac, later led the Jewish people out of slavery in Egypt. God made a new covenant with Moses, providing instructions and rules for living a holy life, including the Ten Commandments.

> According to Jewish tradition, Abraham's first son, Ishmael, is the ancestor of the Arab people. His second son, Isaac, is the ancestor of the Jewish people.

Jews believe that when they follow the Torah—the first five books of the Hebrew Bible, or holy book—and keep God's laws, the Jewish people and the nation of Israel will be blessed by God. They also believe that God will send a Messiah, a political leader chosen by God to bring the

Jewish *exiles* back to Israel, rebuild Jerusalem and restore the Temple that was destroyed by the Romans in 70 C.E., and put an end to the evil in the world. (For more information about Judaism, please see page 108 in Volume 2.)

Christianity

Christianity grew out of Judaism about 2,000 years ago in Israel when Jesus Christ, a Jewish man, began teaching about faith and God's love. Christians believe that Jesus Christ is the son of God, the Messiah sent by God to save people from sin and death. They believe that Jesus was resurrected after his death and that, through faith, they too will have life after death. The Christian Bible includes both the Hebrew Bible (Old Testament) and the teachings of Jesus and his disciples (the New Testament). Unlike Jews and Muslims, Christians believe in the Trinity of God—that God exists as the Father, the Son, and the Holy Spirit. (For more information about Christianity, please see pages 56–60 in Volume 1 of *Discovering World Cultures: The Middle East.*)

Islam

Islam was founded in the seventh century by the Prophet Mohammad, who was a direct descendant of Ishmael. Muslims believe in only one god, Allah, the same god worshiped by Jews and Christians. According to Islamic tradition, Allah's message to humans has been delivered by prophets, such as Abraham, Moses, Jesus, and Mohammad. Holy books, including the Torah, the Christian Gospels, and the Qur'an, preserve the word of Allah. Because the countries in the Middle East are predominantly Islamic, a detailed overview of Islam is provided here.

Basic Beliefs

Muslims believe that the "five pillars of Islam" are the key to salvation:

- *Shahadah:* the acknowledgment that "there is no god but God and that Mohammad is the messenger of God"
- *Salah:* five daily ritual prayers
- *Zakat:* the giving of money to the poor
- *Sawm:* the dawn-to-dusk fast during the month of Ramadan, Islam's most important religious observance
- *Hajj:* the pilgrimage to Mecca, the birthplace of Mohammad

Forms of Islam

About 85 percent of the Islamic community follows the Sunni tradition (in Arabic, *Sunni* refers to the people who follow the sunna, or example, of the prophet). Sunni Muslims believe that the *caliph,* or spiritual leader, should be chosen by the consensus of the Islamic community. They also believe that following *shari'a,* or Islamic, law is essential in living a life that ends in salvation.

The Shi'a tradition teaches that Mohammad appointed his cousin and son-in-law Ali and his descendants to be the spiritual and worldly leaders of Islam after Mohammad's death. Shi'ite (SHE-ite) Muslims believe that these leaders, called *imams,* are free of sin and infallible. About 15 percent of all Muslims follow Shi'a Islam, but there are several different branches within the Shi'a tradition.

Wahhabism is an Islamic reform movement that originated in the eighteenth century in Saudi Arabia. Its members are the most conservative, fundamentalist group in Islam. Members reject any

Iraqi Shi'ite Muslims gather at a holy site in the city of Karbala, Iraq, in April 2003, to mourn the death of one of their most important saints. Under the rule of Iraqi leader Saddam Hussein, they had been banned from observing such rituals for decades. With Hussein's fall from power that same month, however, they were free to worship.

modern interpretations of Islam, including the celebration of Mohammad's birthday or playing music. Muslims who adopt Wahhabi principles label those who don't share their beliefs as infidels or unbelievers, even those who are moderate Sunnis and Shi'ites.

Sources of Muslim Teachings and Tradition

The Qur'an is the only holy book of the Islam faith. Muslims believe that the Qur'an contains the literal word of Allah, or God, which was revealed to the Prophet Mohammad. Memorizing and reciting these holy words is an important part of daily prayer and worship. (Many Americans refer to this book as the Koran, a Westernized spelling of Qur'an.)

While the Qur'an is the only holy text, there are other important spiritual sources in the Islamic faith. The Sunna is a collection of all the stories, sayings, and actions of Mohammad. Followers of Islam use these examples to determine correct behavior in areas not covered in the Qur'an. They often come up with different explanations, which is why customs and beliefs vary sometimes from group to group. One of the distinct features of Islam is the Shari'a, a comprehensive body of laws covering personal, civil, and criminal matters.

COURTESY AND CUSTOMS IN THE MIDDLE EAST

Middle Eastern customs and traditions have developed over centuries, influenced by tribal culture and religion. Visitors to the region should be aware of rules and taboos, such as the ones shown here, that apply in most Middle Eastern countries.

- When greeting a man, clasp his hand briefly without shaking it. A man should never move to shake hands with a woman unless she offers her hand first. Inquiries about an acquaintance's health and interests are expected, but you should never ask about a Muslim's female family members.

- Showing the sole of your shoe to another person, such as when you sit with one leg crossed over the other knee, is very rude. The soles of your shoes should always be pointing downward.

- Always offer and receive items with your right hand. If you are served a meal in a traditional manner, use your right hand for eating (the left hand is regarded as unclean).

- When you visit a person's home, compliments about the home are welcome, but avoid admiring or praising an item excessively. The host may feel obligated to give the item to you as a gift.

- Photographing people is viewed with suspicion in some areas. It is important to ask permission before photographing anyone, especially a woman.

Major Religious Holidays

- *Ashura:* The first ten days of the New Year are a period of mourning for Shi'ite Muslims as they remember the assassination of Hussein, grandson of the Prophet Mohammad, in 680 C.E.

- *Ramadan:* Ramadan honors the time when Mohammad received the first of the Qur'an from Allah. It is the ninth and most holy month in the Islamic year. Muslims do not eat or drink from dawn until dusk during Ramadan. Instead, they reflect on their relationship with Allah, asking for forgiveness for their sins.

- *Eid al-Fitr:* As Ramadan ends, Muslims gather with family and friends to celebrate the feast of Eid al-Fitr. Children often get new clothes for the holiday, which usually lasts three days. Gifts are exchanged among friends and family.

- *Eid al-Adha:* Eid al-Adha (the Feast of the Sacrifice) honors the Prophet Abraham and his devotion to God. At the end of the hajj, the pilgrimage to Mecca, an animal is sacrificed, and the meat is divided between family members and the poor.

A Final Note

Transcribing the Arabic language into English often creates confusion. The two alphabets are very different and there is not a direct correlation of sounds. As a result, Arabic words are often given several different spellings in Western writing. One source may refer to the *emir* of a region, while another labels the ruler an *amir*. The name of the prophet who established Islam appears as Mohammad, Muhammad, and Mohammed. The Islamic holy book is the Qur'an or Koran, and so on. Another source of confusion is the different place names used by Westerners and those who live in the Middle East. For instance, the body of water between Iraq and the Arabian Peninsula has been called the Persian Gulf for centuries by Westerners. People living nearby, however, refer to it as the Arabian Gulf. In this series, the most commonly used spellings and the labels most familiar to Westerners have been used in an effort to avoid confusion. The exception lies in the spelling of *Qur'an*, the Islamic holy book, since scholars as well as many Muslims prefer that spelling over the Westernized *Koran*.

Bahrain

Bahrain (bah-RAIN), the smallest country in the Middle East, is made up of thirty-three islands. It lies just east of Saudi Arabia and west of Qatar (KAH-ter). The largest of the islands is itself called Bahrain and is the home of the country's capital city of Manama. Only six of the islands are inhabited.

Bahrain's location in the Persian Gulf established the island as a vital commercial port in antiquity. This status continues today as Bahrain acts as a link between the Arab and Western worlds. Although Bahrain was one of the first countries to adopt the religion of Islam, its constant exposure to people from other cultures shaped Bahrain into one of the more liberal Islamic countries in the Middle East.

The Bahrainis

As a center of trade, Bahrain has been shaped through the centuries by interactions with many other countries and cultures, especially ancient Mesopotamia. Many native-born Bahrainis are of Arab and Persian ancestry. The influence of the Persians who ruled Bahrain so long ago is still evident in the practice of Shi'a Islam by the majority of Bahrainis and in the Farsi language, which is heard in many Bahraini homes. Although most Bahrainis consider themselves Arab, their culture is

FAST FACTS

✔ **Official name:** Kingdom of Bahrain (also spelled Bahrein)

✔ **Capital:** Manama (ma-NA-muh), also known as Al Manamah

✔ **Location:** Persian Gulf, east of Saudi Arabia

✔ **Area:** 257 square miles (665 square kilometers) (July 2002 estimate)

✔ **Population:** 656,397 (including 228,424 foreign residents)

✔ **Age distribution:**
0–14 years: 29%
15–64 years: 68%
over 65 years: 3%

✔ **Life expectancy:**
Males: 71 years
Females: 76 years

✔ **Ethnic groups:** Bahraini 63%, Asian 19%, other Arab 10%, Iranian 8%

✔ **Religions:** Shi'a Muslim 70%, Sunni Muslim 30%

✔ **Languages:** Arabic, English, Farsi, Urdu

✔ **Currency:**
Bahraini dinar (BHD)
US$1 = 0.38 BHD

✔ **Average annual income:** US$7,640

✔ **Major exports:** Petroleum and petroleum products, aluminum, textiles

Source: CIA, *The World Factbook 2002;*
BBC News Country Profiles.

different in many respects from that of Arabs in Saudi Arabia or Egypt. In recognition of these differences, Bahrainis—along with Arabs from other Persian Gulf nations—are often identified as Gulf Arabs.

The royal Al Khalifa family is directly descended from Arabs who migrated eastward from the Saudi Arabian peninsula in 1701. After winning control of Bahrain from the Persians in 1783, the Al Khalifa family began its uninterrupted rule over Bahrain. The royal family retains close cultural ties with non-Gulf Arabs, following Sunni Islam and speaking Arabic.

The modern Bahraini population is very young, with over half of the native Bahrainis under twenty-one. Because of this, the Bahraini workforce includes many foreigners. Both skilled and unskilled workers come to Bahrain from other countries, drawn by the prospect of wages higher than those in their own countries. Most are from Pakistan, India, and Iran, although a number of Bangladeshi and Filipino workers are also employed in Bahrain. In addition, about 10 percent of Bahrain's foreign residents are from other Arab countries. These foreign-born residents make up more than half of the Bahraini workforce. Overall, the foreign-born residents are a minority, however, making up less than 40 percent of the population. Bahrain is unique among Persian Gulf nations in this respect; Kuwait, Qatar, the United Arab Emirates, and Oman all have more foreign residents than native-born citizens.

> *Bahrain* means "two seas." This refers to fresh water springs that are found in the salty sea off the coast of Bahrain.

The official language of Bahrain is Arabic. However, with so many ethnic groups living in Bahrain, it is not surprising to find that other languages flourish there as well. English is taught in Bahraini schools and is the primary language in business dealings. Farsi and Urdu are also common languages in Bahrain.

Land and Resources

Despite its small size, Bahrain has always played an important role in the Persian Gulf region. Because of its central location and fresh water supply, Bahrain developed into a primary trading center. Today, Bahrain continues in this role, although oil and aluminum have replaced pearls as the leading export and Western countries have become important trading partners.

Geography

The Kingdom of Bahrain is an archipelago—a large group of islands—located in the shallow waters of the Gulf of Bahrain. Of Bahrain's thirty-three islands, only six are inhabited. All together, the islands cover 257 square miles (665 square kilometers), an area about one-fourth the size of Rhode Island.

The largest island, also called Bahrain, is the center of the kingdom. It is about 32 miles (51 kilometers) long and 10 miles (16 kilometers) wide. Most of the island of Bahrain is harsh desert. Limestone outcroppings create rough hills and crevices in the sand-covered terrain. Thorn trees and other desert plants that have adapted to the dry, salty environment dot the landscape. In contrast, date, almond, fig, and pomegranate trees grow along the northern coast, the island's most fertile area.

In the center of the island of Bahrain, the land rises over 400 feet (122 meters) to form an escarpment or cliff called Jabal ad-Dukhan. Its name means "Mountain of Smoke," a reference to the mists that often form around its summit. Most of Bahrain's oil wells are located near Jabal ad-Dukhan.

The other islands in the Bahrain archipelago are desert islands as well, most only a few feet above sea level. Northeast of the island of Bahrain is Al Muharraq, the second largest island. The Bahrain International Airport is located on Al Muharraq. The island of Sitrah—site of Bahrain's main port, a desalination plant, power plant, and oil storage tanks—lies south of

THE TREE OF LIFE

In the desert of southern Bahrain, about 1 mile (1.6 kilometers) from Jabal ad-Dukhan, a lone tree provides welcome shade. Known as the Tree of Life, it is estimated to be 400 years old. The tree's source of water remains a mystery. Some believe that the tree is fed by underground water, but others point out that no other living thing is found in the area surrounding the tree.

Al Muharraq. The royal family's private island—Umm an Nasan—is located west of the island of Bahrain, between Bahrain and Saudi Arabia. Until recently, both Bahrain and Qatar claimed the Hawar Islands near Qatar. In 2001, the International Court of Justice at The Hague ruled that the islands belonged to Bahrain.

Major Cities

Bridges and causeways (roadways built over water) connect the cities on the islands of Bahrain, Al Muharraq, and Sitrah. The 14-mile (22-kilometer) King Fahd Causeway that connects Bahrain with the Saudi Arabian mainland has spurred commercial development and encouraged tourism on the islands since its completion in 1986. Although there are many small villages in Bahrain, about 92 percent of all Bahrainis live in urban areas. The largest cities are Manama and Al Muharraq.

Completely financed by Saudi Arabia, the King Fahd Causeway cost over US$1 billion. The causeway took four years to build. It includes two bridges that allow boats to pass underneath.

Manama

The capital city of Manama, Bahrain's largest city, is located on the northeastern tip of Bahrain Island. Its rapid growth over the past few decades is evident in the ever expanding coastline north of the city. For instance, in the 1940s, the Bab Al Bahrain—the Gateway to Bahrain—was built on the northern coast of Manama. Visitors to Bahrain stepped off boats and walked through the arch as they entered Manama. Today, the famous landmark sits well inside the city of Manama. The sea that it once overlooked is now reclaimed land, filled with towering glass buildings that are home to banks and other international corporations.

The Bab Al Bahrain marks the entrance to Manama's Old *Souk*, or marketplace. The rich aroma of spices fills the air as people wander through narrow, winding streets full of shops. Here, bargain hunters look over displays of items such as clothing, carpets, jewelry, and video recorders. The Cloth Souk is famous for its colorful selection of fabrics, from fine expensive silks to less costly cottons and synthetics, while travelers from around the world visit the Gold Souk to purchase traditional and modern gold jewelry and ornaments.

Manama keeps the past alive for future generations in its museums and cultural centers. The National Museum, which displays artifacts showing 7,000 years of history, is a favorite tourist destination. The Beit Al Qur'an (House of the Qur'an), a center for Qur'anic studies, houses fine examples of Islamic calligraphy and rare manuscripts of the Qur'an. A study center, school, and mosque are also part of the complex. The Heritage Center celebrates traditional Bahraini culture.

Two mosques stand out in the Manama area, vivid contrasts between old and new. Sections of the Masjid al Khamis mosque date back at least 1,000 years. Its twin minarets were added in the fifteenth century. In the newest section of Manama is the enormous Al-Fateh Mosque. Built in the 1990s, it can hold 7,000 worshipers.

To the west of Manama are several interesting archaeological sites. Qal'at Al-Bahrain has extensive excavations. The most recently built fort on the site—the Portuguese Fort—was built in the sixteenth century. The hill that the fort is built upon is actually rubble from previous cities. The oldest layer has been dated to the third millennium B.C.E. Artifacts from the Dilmun, Assyrian, and Portuguese eras have been unearthed at the site. Another site that dates back to the Dilmun period is Barbar, a

The huge Al-Fateh Mosque dominates the view of Manama. Located in the newest section of the city, it was built in the 1990s and can hold thousands of worshipers.

complex of ancient temples. Giant earthen burial mounds southwest of Manama are known as the Royal Tombs. They are the largest mounds found in the kingdom, measuring up to 50 feet (15 meters) high and 150 feet (45 meters) in diameter.

Al Muharraq

A causeway connects Manama to Bahrain's second largest city, Al Muharraq. Al Muharraq is located on the southwestern corner of the island of the same name. It is an older city than Manama, boasting a large souk and homes hundreds of years old. Tourists can visit early homes of the royal family and wealthy pearl merchants, as well as forts built in the sixteenth century. Craftsmen continue the ancient art of boatbuilding at a *dhow* (fishing boat) building yard on the island.

Climate

Bahrain's location near the tropics makes it humid year-round. The summer months of April through October are extremely hot, with temperatures climbing over 100° F (40° C) nearly every day. Temperatures reach their peak in June and July—as high as 125° F (52° C)—when the southwesterly winds known as *qaws* blow across the archipelago. Winters are much more comfortable, with temperatures ranging from 50° to 70° F (10° to 20° C). The humidity often tops 90 percent during the winter months, however, as winds from the southeast—the *shammal*—bring moisture from the gulf over the islands.

Although ancient records indicate that Bahrain was once a lush oasis that beckoned travelers, it has become a desert over the centuries. Erosion contributed to this transformation, as did long periods of drought and the sandstorms created by the *qaws* and *shammal*. Today, Bahrain averages only 3 inches (7.6 centimeters) of rainfall per year.

Natural Resources

Although Bahrain has no rivers or lakes, it does have fresh water in underground aquifers. There are even fresh water springs in the ocean surrounding Bahrain. This bountiful resource in the midst of a desert region was instrumental in the development of Bahrain as an international trading center thousands of years ago. Ships stopped at the island to replenish their stores of fresh water before sailing on to India and other destinations. Today, oil has replaced water as the main reason for the huge ships stopping at Bahrain's ports, but Bahrain's importance to sea trade continues as strong as ever.

The fresh water that is pumped out of the aquifers is used for irrigation as well as for drinking. However, as the fresh water levels fall in the aquifers, saltwater from the Persian Gulf gradually replaces it. The increasingly salty water causes concern for the future of agriculture on the island as well as for the health of Bahraini citizens. As the technology has become available, desalination plants have been built in Bahrain. By 1997, just over half of the fresh water used in Bahrain was from desalination plants.

Until the early twentieth century, the pearling industry contributed greatly to Bahrain's economy. Boats would take divers to offshore oyster beds where they would make about fifty dives a day during the four-month pearling season. Sharks, poisonous snakes, and malnutrition made a diver's life dangerous. The pearling industry collapsed in the 1930s when Japan introduced cultured (artificial) pearls into the world market.

A Bahraini fisherman opens a shell looking for pearls at a fish market in Manama. Although pearls are no longer an important part of the economy of Bahrain, they are still a national icon and are sold in small numbers by jewelers. Images of pearls are also used in public statues around the island.

As the market for pearls declined another natural resource—oil—rose to prominence. Although oil had been discovered in 1902, it wasn't until 1932 that the first successful well was established. Although the petroleum and natural gas reserves found on Bahrain are small in comparison to others in the Middle East, the income from this resource has changed the lives of all Bahrainis. Experts predict that the reserves will be depleted between 2005 and 2010. This news has led the Bahraini government to invest in more sustainable industries, such as petroleum refineries and aluminum smelters.

Plants and Animals

The desert climate of Bahrain has limited the plant and animal life on the islands. Plants, such as the desert shrubs and palm trees found across the island, must be very hardy and able to tolerate dry, salty conditions.

Few large animals run wild on Bahrain's islands. Scorpions, snakes, hares, and hedgehogs are more likely to survive the harsh environment. Birds are found in great numbers; many are migratory birds that winter in the islands.

Desert Refuge

The Al-Areen Wildlife Park and Reserve, located on the main island of Bahrain, is dedicated to the conservation of the Arabian oryx and other indigenous Arabian animals. Its goal is to protect endangered desert species through the establishment of breeding programs.

History

Ancient Days

Archaeologists have found evidence that people were living on Bahrain 50,000 years ago, but not much is known about the earliest inhabitants. As farming practices developed on Bahrain, about 8,000 years ago, people were able to establish settlements in the region.

Bahrain owes its early importance to the fact that early civilizations in Mesopotamia (present-day Iraq) lacked resources such as copper and lumber. The Sumerians who lived in Mesopotamia began sailing through the Persian Gulf to the Arabian Peninsula and the Indus Valley (present-day Pakistan), where they traded their food products for the goods they needed. Cities along their route developed into trading centers and way stations where sailors could stock up on fresh water and trade their goods. Dilmun, located on Bahrain, emerged as one of the most vital of these ancient trading cities in the fourth millennium B.C.E.

IMPORTANT EVENTS IN BAHRAIN'S HISTORY

6000 B.C.E. First people settle in Bahrain.

2200 B.C.E. Dilmun civilization controls trading routes within the Persian Gulf.

1000 B.C.E. Dilmun's importance declines as overland travel improves.

600 B.C.E. Dilmun regains importance as part of the Assyrian Empire.

323 B.C.E. Greek Seleucids dominate Persian Gulf; Dilmun becomes known as Tylos.

250 B.C.E. Parthian dynasty comes to power in the Persian Gulf.

226 C.E. Sassanids take over Persian Empire from the Parthians.

628 Byzantine Empire conquers Sassanids and adds Bahrain to its lands.

661 Bahrainis convert to Islam and become part of the Umayyad Caliphate.

750 Abbasid Caliphate succeeds the Umayyads.

1521 Portuguese claim ownership of Bahrain.

1602 Portuguese forced out of Bahrain by Iran.

1783 Al Khalifa family—ancestors of today's ruling family—gains control over Bahrain.

1820 Britain signs treaties with Persian Gulf states to end piracy in the region.

1861 Bahrain becomes a British protectorate; pearling industry booms.

1902 Bahrainis discover oil.

1929 Japanese develop cultured pearls, Bahrain's pearling industry rapidly declines.

1932 Oil production begins.

1935 First oil refinery is built.

1942 Sheikh Salman bin Hamad Al Khalifa rules Bahrain.

1949 Bahrain becomes headquarters for U.S. Middle East forces.

1961 Sheikh Isa bin Salman Al Khalifa becomes head of state.

1968 Britain announces that protectorate relationship with Bahrain and other Persian Gulf states will end in 1971.

1970 Iran relinquishes claim to Bahrain following UN-sponsored election to determine Bahrain's preferences.

1971 Independence from Britain on August 15; Bahrain joins the United Nations (UN) and the Arab League; Sheikh Isa bin Salman Al Khalifa becomes emir.

1973 First constitution calls for elected representatives to form a legislative body—the National Assembly.

1975 The emir suspends the National Assembly; Shi'ite majority lodges strong protests. Companies establish offshore banking.

1979 Iranian Revolution brings Shi'ite majority to power in Iran.

1981 Persian Gulf states form the Gulf Cooperation Council (GCC) for mutual protection. Bahraini military prevents the planned overthrow of the government by Iranian-backed Shi'ite militants.

1986 Newly completed King Fahd Causeway links Saudi Arabia and Bahrain.

1990 Iraq invades Kuwait. Bahrain joins allied forces fighting against Iraq, offers military bases and support services to the American and British troops fighting in the Gulf War (Desert Storm).

1994 Shi'ite protesters demand that the National Assembly be reinstated.

1999 Crown Prince Hamad bin Isa Al Khalifa becomes emir following his father's death and proposes radical reforms to Bahrain's constitution.

2002 Bahrainis support change from a kingdom to a constitutional monarchy. Emir Hamad bin Isa Al Khalifa becomes Bahrain's first king.

2003 Bahrain provides support for coalition forces during war against Iraq.

Dilmun

By 2200 B.C.E., Dilmun was firmly established as a trading center of great importance. At the height of its power, from 2200 B.C.E. to 1600 B.C.E., Dilmun controlled the Persian Gulf trading routes, becoming very wealthy. Fortified cities and elaborate temples were built. Dilmun also became very important as a burial ground, possibly because it was a center of trade with a large population or because the Sumerians and other ancient Mesopotamians considered it a holy paradise.

Around 1000 B.C.E., trade in the region began shifting from copper to spices and incense. At the same time, the domestication of the camel made overland trading routes feasible. These developments led to a gradual decline in Dilmun's importance. The increase in overland trading also brought more Arab settlers to Bahrain.

A Prize for Conquerors

Throughout the first millennium B.C.E., powerful empires battled each other for control of the Middle Eastern region. Bahrain, like other countries in the Persian Gulf, fell under the control of several different empires during this period.

HEAVEN ON EARTH

In ancient times, the Sumerians considered Dilmun to be paradise, a place where the strong and righteous enjoyed eternal life. One Sumerian story told of a great flood that destroyed the earth and the people who lived there, a story very similar to the Old Testament story of Noah. In the Sumerian version, one man was chosen to survive the disaster. Because of his goodness, the gods gave him the gift of immortality and sent him to live in Dilmun, a paradise in which there is no illness or aging.

Over 150,000 burial mounds have been found on Bahrain, lending credence to archaeologists' belief that ancient people considered it a holy site. The abundant fresh water found on Bahrain and the extensive pearl oyster beds around the islands also lead historians and archaeologists to believe that the ancient land of Dilmun was located here. Some have even theorized that Bahrain was the site of the Garden of Eden.

These ancient ruins are at Saar, just outside of Manama. The island of Bahrain has many such ruins and ancient burial sites.

Toward the end of the fourth century B.C.E., the Macedonian conqueror Alexander the Great sent Greek ships to explore the Persian Gulf region. (Macedonia is located in present-day Greece.) Alexander died before he could add Dilmun to his empire, but his successors—the Seleucids—dominated the region for several decades. During this period, the main island was known by its Greek name, Tylos. The Greek influence is apparent in the pottery, glassware, and jewelry that were produced then.

The Parthians, a Persian *dynasty,* came to power in the region about 250 B.C.E. They added the countries of the Persian Gulf to their empire in order to control the trading routes, establishing military posts in Bahrain and other gulf countries. In the third century C.E., control of the Persian Empire passed to the Sassanids, another Persian dynasty. Bahrain remained under Persian control until the seventh century C.E., when the Byzantine Empire briefly took control of the Persian Gulf.

With the rise of Islam in the seventh century, the caliph, *or spiritual leader, became an important figure in Bahrain and neighboring Arabia. At that time, the* caliphs *ruled from Iraq.*

The Islamic Dynasties

The religion of Islam began in 610 in the western part of Arabia, when Mohammad began preaching and sharing revelations that Muslims believe were given to him by God. Bahrain, with close ties to neighboring Arabia, was one of the first countries to embrace Islam. During the Umayyad (661–750) and Abbasid (750–1258) dynasties, the *caliph*—the Islamic ruler and spiritual leader—ruled from what is now Iraq. Trade in the Persian Gulf flourished once more, and Bahrain's ports and markets thrived.

The Europeans Arrive

In the fifteenth century, the Portuguese made their way along the coast of Africa in search of new routes to India. Their ultimate success gave the Portuguese control of new trading routes that enabled them to bypass the Persian Gulf region and deal directly with India. By the early sixteenth century, the Portuguese established forts in the Persian Gulf and controlled the lucrative trade routes in that region. The Portuguese occupied Bahrain by 1521, controlling the island for over eighty years.

The Bahrainis chafed under European rule, and in 1602, a group of rebels seized the Portuguese fort. They called upon neighboring Iran (Persia) for help. After defeating the Portuguese, Iran ruled over the islands for nearly 200 years.

The Al Khalifa

In the mid-1700s, nomadic tribes from the central Arabian Peninsula began to migrate to the Persian Gulf coast, drawn by better economic conditions. The Al Khalifa family, Sunni Muslims of the Bani Utub tribe, made their way to Qatar, where they soon gained control over parts of the region. Using Qatar as a base, the Al Khalifa family pushed the Iranians out of Bahrain in 1783 and established themselves as the ruling family on the islands. Their descendants still rule Bahrain today.

About this same time, Britain and the Netherlands were actively trading in the area. The British became more powerful and, in the early 1800s, began signing treaties with the gulf states. Initially meant to end piracy in the gulf and make trading routes safer, the treaties

Arab tribal society is based on family ties. The name of the tribe usually refers to an ancestor or an event in the past. *Bani Utub,* the tribe to which the Al Khalifa family belongs, can be translated as "sons of wanderers." They were given this name after they moved, or wandered, from the deserts of Arabia to the Persian Gulf region in 1744.

expanded in scope until—a century later—Britain essentially controlled the foreign policy of Bahrain and other countries in the Persian Gulf. In further treaties, Britain promised protection against stronger, neighboring countries, such as Saudi Arabia. Bahrain became a British *protectorate,* or protected state, in 1861.

The Discovery of Oil

Oil was discovered in 1902, and as the pearling industry began its decline in the 1930s, Bahrain became the first Persian Gulf country to exploit its oil reserves. While the petroleum reserves weren't large, they helped Bahrain continue its prosperity. The discovery of oil also led to conflict as Saudi Arabia, Iraq, and Iran all claimed territory in the Persian Gulf. It was Iran's claim of ownership of Bahrain that ultimately caused the most distress, however.

Bahrain's ruling family used the income from petroleum sales to build roads, develop the water supply, and provide social services such as education and free health care. They replaced tribal councils with a modern government structure that led to increased commercial opportunities. Because of this modern approach to business and

PEARLS OF GREAT BEAUTY

From the ninth century through the early twentieth century, pearls from Bahrain's oyster beds were prized for their lustrous beauty and size. As British influence expanded in the Persian Gulf, the pearling industry grew. By the early 1900s, about 900 ships were involved in the pearling industry. Nearly half of all Bahraini men depended upon pearls for their income, either as ship captains, divers who harvested the pearls, or pearl traders.

As the 1930s' economic depression hit Europe, the sale of luxury items such as pearls declined. Before the economy could rebound, Japan introduced cultured pearls to the world. These mass-produced pearls were much cheaper than the real thing, and soon the market for Bahraini pearls dwindled to unsustainable levels. Today, most of the

pearls harvested in Bahrain's waters are sold to tourists. Visitors to Bahrain can even take scuba diving trips to the pearl beds and try their luck at finding their own pearls.

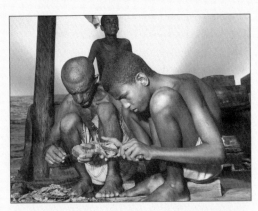

Pearls are still harvested in small quantities in the waters off Bahrain and sold mainly to tourists. Visitors can also dive in search of their own pearls.

government, the British established their regional naval headquarters in Bahrain.

An Independent Country

In 1968, Britain announced that—as a cost-cutting measure—the gulf state protectorates would end in 1971. Bahrain, Qatar, and the present-day United Arab Emirates (UAE) considered forming a federation, but negotiations were unsuccessful. Iran stepped forward once more to claim ownership of Bahrain. A UN-sponsored election in 1970 allowed Bahrainis to vote on the issue. An overwhelming majority chose independence over union with Iran, causing Iran to withdraw its claim.

Prior to the discovery of oil, the boundaries of Persian Gulf states were loosely defined. A strong nomadic heritage and desert climate made boundaries relatively unimportant. Once oil was discovered, however, firm boundaries were a necessity in determining who benefited from the precious resource.

On August 15, 1971, Bahrain became an independent state, ruled by Emir Isa bin Salman Al Khalifa (EE-sah bihn SUHL-mahn al kah-LEE-fah). A new constitution was approved in 1973, calling for the creation of a legislative body called the National Assembly. Problems arose almost immediately as the National Assembly and the emir's cabinet advisers disagreed on one issue after another. The emir finally suspended the assembly in 1975, a move resented by the Shi'ite majority who were left without a voice in government.

Conflicts in Iran and Iraq in the late 1970s and early 1980s worried the small countries in the Persian Gulf, including Bahrain. The 1979 Iranian Revolution brought the Ayatollah Khomeini, a Shi'ite Muslim

THE GULF COOPERATION COUNCIL

The instability that rocked the gulf region following the Iranian Revolution underscored the vulnerability of the small gulf states. In 1981, Bahrain, Kuwait, Oman, UAE, Qatar, and Saudi Arabia formed the Gulf Cooperation Council (GCC). The members of the GCC established a regional defense policy and collaborate on economic and trade issues. Although the GCC has strengthened the military in the gulf region, member countries still rely heavily on the West—especially Britain and the United States—for extra protection.

This protection became necessary in the mid-1980s during the Iran-Iraq War, when Iran was poised to attack Kuwaiti oil tankers in the Persian Gulf, and again in 1991, during the Gulf War. Throughout both conflicts, Bahrain provided key naval support for U.S. and other Western forces. The United States and Bahrain remain close allies today, with Bahrain providing a support base for American naval forces in the Middle East.

leader, to power in Iran. (*Ayatollah* is a title used by Shi'ite Muslims to refer to religious leaders.) Other countries with a large Shi'ite population worried that the revolution would spread. In the early 1980s, in the midst of the Iran-Iraq War, several explosions occurred in Bahrain. They were attributed to Shi'ite Muslims who sympathized with—and were possibly supported by—Iran.

Bahrain Today

The 1990s were marked by growing unrest among Bahrain's Shi'ite population. Although Shi'ite Muslims are in the majority in Bahrain, the ruling family and most government leaders are Sunni Muslims. Protests were staged in the mid-1990s to demand that the National Assembly be reinstated. Negotiations failed, and the unrest continued throughout the end of the decade.

In 1999, Hamad bin Isa Al Khalifa (HAH-mahd bihn EE-sah al kah-LEE-fah) was named emir following the death of his father. He began implementing a series of reforms aimed at improving relations with the Shi'ite population. The reforms included the release of political prisoners and a proposal to change Bahrain into a constitutional monarchy that

THE FIRST KING OF BAHRAIN

Sheikh Hamad bin Isa Al Khalifa is the first member of Bahrain's ruling family to bear the title of king. Before 2001, Bahrain was an emirate—an Islamic country ruled by a prince or chieftain—and Sheikh Hamad had the title of emir. In 2001, Bahrainis approved a proposal by Sheikh Hamad to make Bahrain a constitutional monarchy. In this form of government, a king rules over the country, but representation of the various groups within that country is provided by a legislative body composed of at least some democratically elected members.

Before becoming king of Bahrain, Sheikh Hamad attended military officer training schools in England and the United States. Upon his return to Bahrain, he founded the Bahrain Defense Force and served as minister of defense from 1971 to 1988. Following his father's death in 1999, Sheikh

Hamad became Bahrain's emir and the supreme commander of the Bahrain Defense Force. As emir, he launched a series of reforms that resulted in the creation of Bahrain's constitutional monarchy.

In a step toward democracy, Sheikh Hamad bin Isa Al Khalifa officially became king of the new constitutional monarchy known as the Kingdom of Bahrain in February 2002.

would be ruled by a king and a partially elected legislative body. Another major reform was giving women the right to vote and run for office. A vote in 2001 showed overwhelming support for the changes among the Bahraini population. A year later, legislative elections were held. Although several women ran for office, none were elected. While most Bahrainis are pleased that the National Assembly has been restored, some are still pushing for a fully elected legislative body.

Economy

Bahrain's economy has always been one of the strongest in the Persian Gulf region. The importance of the merchant class throughout Bahrain's history helped establish a culture that values business and wealth.

Business and Industry

A major center of trade from its earliest days, Bahrain also had a thriving shipbuilding industry and fishing trade. The pearling industry contributed greatly to the economy from ancient times until the early 1930s. Fortunately, oil was discovered in the kingdom about the time that the pearling industry declined. Petroleum production and refineries have since been the major source of Bahrain's income, but the oil reserves are limited. Experts believe that they could be depleted as early as 2005.

Anticipating the time when oil income ceases, the Bahraini government has moved to diversify the economy. Rather than relying upon its own meager oil reserves for income, Bahrain enlarged its refinery and port facilities to process and ship oil from throughout the gulf region, enabling the small country to become the major oil supplier in the area. In addition, the natural gas that is found in the oil reserves is now captured and processed to provide butane, naphtha, and propane.

Although the oil industry remains under the control of the government, private companies run the fast-growing banking sector. In the 1970s, when a civil war in Lebanon disrupted the role of Beirut as the major banking center of the Middle East, Bahrain acted swiftly, establishing itself as the new financial hub of the region. Today, Bahrain is recognized as an important player in the international banking system.

Aluminum processing is another industry that was established to diversify the economy. In the 1960s, Bahrain experienced a period of rising unemployment. To provide jobs, the government built an aluminum smelting plant. The plant is powered by natural gas produced in Bahrain. It refines bauxite (aluminum ore) from Australia and sells the finished product in Asia and the West. After several expansions, Aluminum Bahrain (ALBA) ranks as one of the largest aluminum smelters in the world.

In the past few decades, Bahrain's newest industry—tourism—has grown enormously. Visitors to Bahrain can explore archaeological sites and dive for pearls. The souks, or markets, offer exotic goods that remind visitors of Bahrain's location at the crossroads of many different civilizations and cultures. Trips to the Heritage Center—sponsored by the government—and to rural villages provide a glimpse of a rapidly disappearing way of life.

This artist's rendering shows the plan for a huge financial complex to be constructed in the old Manama seaport. Demonstrating Bahrain's prominence in Middle Eastern finance, the construction was planned to begin in late 2003 and take six years to complete.

Media and Communications

Given Bahrain's reputation as a cosmopolitan center, it is no surprise to find modern communications and media offerings widely available. Up-to-date fiber-optic telephone networks are common in urban areas, and use of cellular phones is widespread. Satellite stations provide reliable international connections.

Radio and television stations provide news and entertainment to Bahrainis. By 1998, Bahrain had five radio stations and four television stations. About half the population owns a radio, while 42 percent own television sets. An Internet service provider in Bahrain serves about 100,000 computer users.

Religion and Beliefs

During the Persian era (250 B.C.E. to 650 C.E.), Judaism, Christianity, and Zoroastrianism were introduced to Bahrain. Some Arabs adopted Judaism and Christianity; Zoroastrianism was practiced mainly by Persian (Iranian) settlers. (To learn more about Christianity, see pages 56–60 in this volume. For information about Zoroastrianism and Judaism, please see pages 27 and 108–109, respectively, in Volume 2 of this series.)

Islam was introduced in the Persian Gulf region in the seventh century. While most Bahrainis embraced Islam, a small number maintained their Jewish or Christian traditions. Today, Islam is the official religion of Bahrain, and about 85 percent of the population is Muslim. Bahrainis have the freedom to follow any religion, however. About 7 percent of the Bahraini population, mostly foreign residents, follow Christianity. The remaining 8 percent, also mostly foreigners, are practicing Hindus, Buddhists, and Jews.

Islam

Muslims follow the teachings of the Prophet Mohammad, who established Islam in the seventh century. They believe in one God—Allah—who revealed the Qur'an to Mohammad, the last in a series of prophets that includes Abraham and Jesus. Devout Muslims observe the five pillars of Islam: professing that "there is no God but God and Mohammad is his messenger," praying five times daily, fasting during the holy month of Ramadan, giving alms (charity) to the poor, and making a pilgrimage to Mecca, the birthplace of Mohammad. (To learn more about Islam, see pages 87–88 in this volume.)

Within the Muslim community in Bahrain, there are two major groups. The ruling family and most merchants are Sunni Muslims, the most prevalent group within Islam. The majority of Bahraini Muslims— about 70 percent—follow Shi'a tradition. The Shi'ites tend to be poorer and have fewer opportunities for advancement than their Sunni counterparts, which has led to political tension and dissent over the years.

Everyday Life

Bahraini culture is based on Arab tribal customs as well as the principles of Islam. The ongoing interaction with people from many different countries and cultures, however, results in a more open, cosmopolitan society than is found in many other Islamic countries.

Family Life

As in other Islamic countries, the family is the center of society in Bahrain. Men and women generally follow the gender roles prescribed by religion and custom, although these roles are interpreted more liberally in Bahrain than in Saudi Arabia and other conservative Islamic countries. More women are taking advantage of educational opportunities than ever before. These well-educated women play an ever more important role in the workplace. At the same time, many of the women who live in rural areas continue to follow the same traditions as their mothers and grandmothers, staying in the home to care for their families.

The Qur'an allows a Muslim man to take up to four wives, as long as he can support them all in a similar manner. Today, however, few Bahraini men marry more than one woman. The men do retain their role of authority in most families, though, especially in conservative, rural Shi'ite families.

Bahraini children are loved and indulged by their parents and other relatives. They typically live with their families until they marry. Traditionally, marriages were arranged by the bride and groom's parents because young people were not allowed to date. While arranged marriages still occur, today's prospective marriage partners have a much greater degree of control over the process. Neither men nor women are forced to marry someone they don't care for.

Dress

Bahraini men and women are expected to dress modestly and avoid exposing the body. Adults generally wear traditional clothing, although it is becoming more common to see Western suits and dresses in Manama and, to a lesser degree, Al Muharraq. Women may wear Western-style clothing in the workplace, but long sleeves are preferred. In contrast to more conservative Islamic countries, Bahraini women are allowed to appear in public with their heads, faces, and hands uncovered.

A Bahraini girl wears an elaborately decorated traditional daffa *(headpiece) and* thawb *(robe), most likely for a special occasion.*

Women wearing traditional clothing don a *thawb* (THA-oob), a robe of cotton or silk, over a loose undergarment. Thawbs are often brightly colored and highly decorated with embroidery. Those worn for special occasions such as weddings are often decorated with gold and silver. The *daffa* (DAH-fah), also embroidered with complex designs, covers the head but leaves the face uncovered. Those women who want to be covered completely in public wear a *milfa* (MILL-fah), which has a net-like covering that can be lowered over the face.

Traditional dress for men is a *thawb* (THA-oob), a long white cotton robe with long sleeves but no collar. A *ghutra* (GHOO-truh), or headcloth, is held in place with a length of white or black cord called an *agal* (ah-GAHL). In the winter, men may wear a woolen robe, or *bisht* (bihsht), rather than a *thawb*. Outer garments or cloaks are often made of camel hair.

Education

In 1919, Bahrain became the first country in the Persian Gulf region to establish a public school for boys. Ten years later, a girls' school opened. Today, school attendance is required for all children between the ages of six and fifteen. As a result, Bahrainis are highly educated, with one of the highest literacy rates—89 percent—in the Middle East. Many Bahraini youth continue their education at the College of Health Sciences and the University of Bahrain, which opened in Manama in 1976 and 1986 respectively. Many children from wealthy families pursue a university education in the United States or the United Kingdom.

The public education system is provided free of charge to all Bahraini children. The cost of everything, including transportation, books, uniforms, and meals, is paid by the government. Children attend six years of primary school, three years of intermediate school, and three years of secondary school. Whenever possible, separate schools are provided for boys and girls. In small villages with only one school, the day is split up. Boys attend for half the day; then the girls take their turn. All children attend school from Saturday to Wednesday. Their weekend occurs on Thursday and Friday (the Islamic holy day).

Besides the public schools, many private schools are available in Bahrain. Some of these offer a religious education while others serve the communities of foreign residents who work in Bahrain.

Recreation and Leisure

Bahrainis enjoy a wide variety of leisure activities, including horse racing, organized sports, and desert camping. Arabian horses, the most ancient breed of horse, have been prized by people in the Arabian Peninsula for centuries. According to tradition, Ishmael, the son of Abraham and ancestor of Mohammad, was the first to tame the Arabian horse. Today, many wealthy Bahrainis own and race Arabian thoroughbreds. Riding schools and clubs are very popular.

The influence of Western cultures shows up in Bahraini sports. Cricket, a game similar to baseball that originated in Britain, is played by many Bahraini residents. Tennis, squash, and golf are also popular. Bahrain's favorite organized sport, however, may be soccer.

The ancestors of many native Bahrainis were nomadic Arabs who lived in the desert. Today, many families enjoy spending the weekend camping in the desert. Extended families pitch their tents and visit with one another as the children play.

Bahraini children today enjoy many of the same activities as their counterparts in the United States and Europe, including video games and amusement parks. However, they still enjoy traditional activities. Girls often play *al-kerdiyah*, a game in which they use rag dolls to act out stories. Boys may race small boats that they have made or play marbles. All children enjoy playing hide-and-seek.

From horseracing to cricket, many sports are enjoyed in Bahrain. But the most popular, as it is the world over, is probably soccer.

Food

The rich cultural background of the Bahraini people is apparent in its cuisine. Traditional Bahraini dishes make use of a wide variety of foods that are readily available on the islands, including fish, lamb, rice, and dates. Arab foods, such as falafel (fried ground chickpeas served with vegetables in pita bread) and *shawarma* (roasted lamb or chicken wrapped in flat bread), acknowledge Bahrain's shared heritage. Delicately spiced foods invoke Bahrain's past as a trading center on the India spice route, while restaurants serving foods from all over the world emphasize Bahrain's modern status as an international city.

Did You Know?

Dates grown in Bahrain are considered to be the sweetest and most delicious of all dates.

Many of the fruits and vegetables eaten in Bahrain are grown on the islands. Dates, bananas, mangoes, pomegranates, cucumbers, and tomatoes are all cultivated locally. While some livestock is raised for food, most meat is imported from other countries. Fish and shrimp are readily available, caught daily off Bahrain's coast by local fishermen.

SEMAK BI SALSIT AL KARRY

(CURRIED FISH WITH DRIED LIME)

Bahrain was a center for the spice trade with India for centuries, and many Bahraini residents today are from India and Pakistan. Curries such as these are very popular in Bahrain and other countries in the Persian Gulf.

2 onions, chopped
2 tablespoons olive oil
2 cloves garlic, minced
Salt to taste
1 teaspoon curry powder
1/2 cinnamon stick
3 tomatoes, peeled and chopped
2 cups water or chicken stock
1 *loomi**
1-1/4 pounds fish fillets (or 2-1/2 pounds whole fish)

Sauté the onions in the olive oil until softened. Add the garlic, salt, and curry powder. Cook for another minute. Stir in the cinnamon stick, tomatoes, and water. Cover and simmer 5 minutes.

Add the loomi to the pot. Gently place the fish into the sauce, then cover the pot. Poach the fish over low heat until it is tender and flaky. (The time will vary depending upon the thickness of the fillets, but 10 minutes per inch of thickness is a good rule of thumb.)

Serves 4.

**Loomi* are dried limes that are used throughout the Persian Gulf region. They can be found in many Middle Eastern markets in the United States.

Source: Adapted from *The Arabian Delights Cookbook* by Anne Marie Weiss-Armush.

Bahrainis, like other Arabs, enjoy a tradition of drinking coffee. Bahraini coffee is prepared with cardamom, saffron, and rosewater and served in small cups. Traditional courtesy requires guests to accept a second cup of coffee if one is offered. After that, however, a guest can refuse another cup by shaking the cup from side to side.

Holidays and Festivals

With the exception of National Day on December 16, which celebrates the end of the British protectorate system, Bahraini holidays are related to the Islamic calendar.

Ramadan, the month during which Muslims fast from sunrise to sunset, is one of the most significant religious observances in the Islamic world. The self-discipline required for the fast shows one's devotion to Allah, while experiencing hunger and thirst encourages empathy for those who are poor and hungry all year long. As Ramadan ends, Muslims celebrate Eid al-Fitr, a three-day holiday full of feasting, visiting, and gift exchanges.

The *hajj*, or pilgrimage to the holy city of Mecca, is one of the highlights of every Muslim's life. At the end of the hajj, Muslims celebrate Eid al-Adha. This holiday generally lasts three or four days. It commemorates Abraham's willingness to sacrifice his son to God. Families sacrifice one of their sheep or goats and share the meat with the less fortunate in their community. Then they roast the remaining meat and enjoy a feast with friends and family members.

Shi'ite Muslims observe Ashura during the first ten days of the Islamic New Year. This solemn period of mourning marks the anniversary of the assassination of Mohammad's grandson Hussein in 680 C.E.

The Arts

The expression of heritage, experience, and emotion through art is well developed in Bahrain. From traditional crafts through modern performance art, Bahrain offers a vital, creative art scene.

Traditional Crafts

Bahrain's past as a commercial trading center led to the development of many traditional items whose products the Bahraini people sold or bartered. Once neglected and on the verge of dying out, traditional crafts are enjoying a renaissance today. Some villages specialize in a particular craft. Thus, Bani Jamrah is known for its weaving, A'ali for its pottery, and Karbabad for its baskets. Artisans in Manama and Al Muharraq continue to build *dhows*, traditional Arab ships, using time-proven methods.

The Al Jasra Handicraft Center opened in 1990 in the coastal village of Al Jasra with a goal of preserving crafts that, in years past, had their own *souks*, or markets, in Bahrain's towns and cities. Today's artisans use traditional skills and designs to carve wooden chests, make pottery, and weave textiles. These crafts, which began as a way to earn income for the family, are now encouraged as a means of preserving a proud heritage.

These intricately carved wooden doors are an example of the traditional crafts that can be found at Bahrain's Al Jasra Handicraft Center. Modern-day artisans create these objects using the same traditional designs and techniques as their ancestors. Years ago, many of these crafts were featured at their own souks, *or markets.*

Visual Arts

Islam restricts artists from creating representations of living creatures. Muslims believe that whoever does this is aspiring to compete with Allah, the creator of life. Instead, Islamic art features intricate geometric decorations called *arabesque*. Calligraphy, or beautiful writing, is also an important art form in Islamic countries. Verses from the Qur'an are often inscribed as decoration upon objects or walls.

The Beit Al Qur'an, or House of the Qur'an, is a unique museum in Bahrain. Dedicated to the Islamic holy book, the site includes a mosque, a museum, and a study center. Calligraphy adorns the walls of the buildings. Rare and valuable copies of the Qur'an are exhibited in the museum.

Contemporary, modern art thrives in Bahrain as well. Painters, sculptors, and photographers create narrative as well as abstract art that illuminates life in Bahrain.

Performing Arts

A wide range of performing arts is offered in Bahrain, typically in concert halls, museums, and outdoor arenas near Manama. The Bahrain Orchestra for Arab Music performs frequently at the Bahrain National Museum. Classical ballet and other dance productions inspire many young Bahrainis to study Western dances such as ballet, modern, jazz, tap, and Irish dance.

Music in Bahrain is unique to the region. It combines musical influences from many different countries, including Saudi Arabia, India, and Iran. Bedouin songs set poetry and stories to melodies. Singers are accompanied by percussion instruments such as the *tar* or frame drum. Another style of folk music originated with the pearl divers. Away from home and living on a boat for the four-month pearling season, the divers followed the lead of a hired singer. Their songs marked the different tasks that needed to be completed, such as setting sail and approaching the pearl banks.

Tourists frequent nightclubs that offer everything from pop music and disco to traditional Arabian tunes. Modern movie theaters, like the nightclubs, attract more tourists than local Bahraini residents.

Literature

Poetry has a long history in Bahrain, and poets are well respected. Writers such as Ibrahima Al-Urayyid and Ahmad Muhammad Al Khalifa create classical Arabic poetry that extols romance and beauty. Many younger writers explore political issues in their poetry and novels.

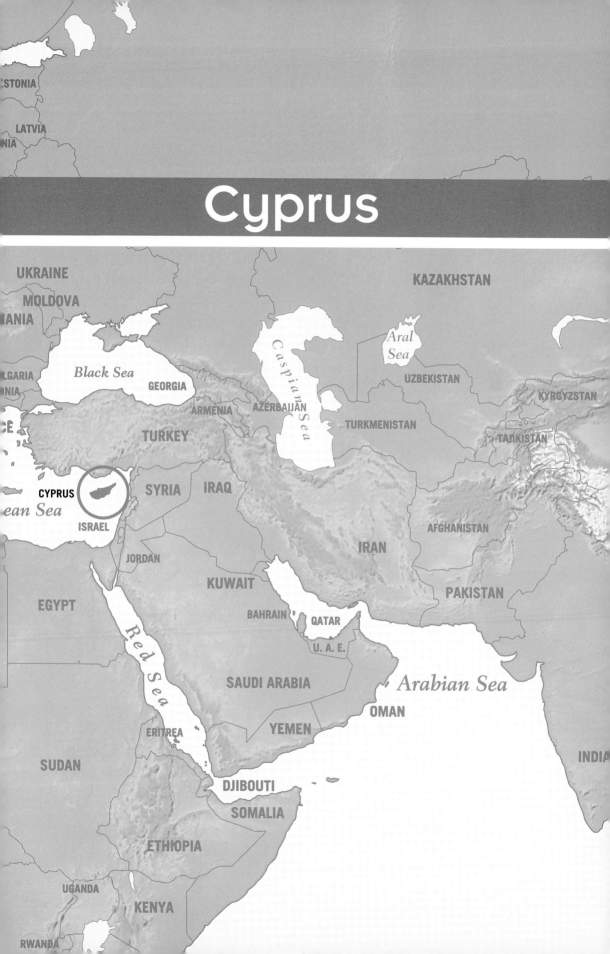

Cyprus

Located in the eastern Mediterranean at the crossroads of Europe, Asia, and Africa, the small island of Cyprus has played a large role in world history. Lying south of Turkey and west of Syria, Cyprus quickly became an important trading center. Leaders of ancient empires, drawn by the rich deposits of copper and the dense forests, conquered Cyprus and plundered its resources. Medieval knights from Western Europe stopped in Cyprus on their way to and from the Crusades. Today, the island's historical past as well as its modern conveniences draw tourists from around the world.

Cyprus was called the "island of love" by the ancient Greeks, who believed that Aphrodite, the Greek goddess of love and beauty, was born there. In modern times, however, Cyprus has been subject to hate, enduring a period of violence and strife between its two major ethnic groups—Greek and Turkish Cypriots—that resulted in the *partition*, or division, of the island in 1974.

Today, nearly all Greek Cypriots live in the southern two-thirds of the island that is governed by the Republic of Cyprus. Turkish Cypriots declared the northern region to be an independent country—the Turkish Republic of Northern Cyprus (TRNC)—in 1983. However, the TRNC has not been recognized as an independent nation by any country except Turkey. Following the failure of reunification talks

FAST FACTS

✔ **Official name:** Republic of Cyprus (Turkish Cypriots call their area the Turkish Republic of Northern Cyprus)

✔ **Capital:** Nicosia (also known as Lefkosia and Lefkosa)

✔ **Location:** Mediterranean Sea, south of Turkey

✔ **Area:** 3,571 square miles (9,250 square kilometers)

✔ **Population:** 767,314 (July 2002 estimate)

✔ **Age distribution:**
0–14 years: 22.4%
15–64 years: 66.6%
over 65 years: 11%

✔ **Life expectancy:**
Males: 75 years
Females: 80 years

✔ **Ethnic groups:** Greek 85%, Turkish 12%, other 3%

✔ **Religions:** Greek Orthodox 78%, Muslim 18%, other 4%

✔ **Languages:** Greek, Turkish, English

✔ **Currency:**
Greek Cypriot area: Cypriot pound (CYP)
US$1 = 0.55 Cypriot pounds (2003)
Turkish Cypriot area: Turkish lira (TRL)
US$1 = 1,645,221.18 TRL

✔ **Average annual income:** US$11,950

✔ **Major exports:** Citrus fruit, potatoes, grapes, wine, cement, textiles, clothing, shoes

Source: CIA, *The World Factbook 2002*;
BBC News Country Profiles.

sponsored by the United Nations (UN) in early 2003, it appears that the two regions of the country will remain separate entities.

The Cypriots

The people of Cyprus are famous for their hospitality to strangers, which makes it all the more ironic that many Cypriots have never spoken to their neighbors who belong to the opposite ethnic group. The people of Cyprus, like the island itself, are divided by ethnicity. Despite religious and ethnic differences, earlier generations of Greek and Turkish Cypriots did mingle in towns and villages throughout Cyprus. This began to change in the late nineteenth century when the push for *enosis*—union with Greece—began to take shape. The differences between the Greek and Turkish Cypriots deepened when the British took control of the island in 1878. Under British rule, the educational system and the government were divided along ethnic lines. Greece supplied textbooks and educational direction to the Greek Cypriots while Turkey did the same for the Turkish Cypriots. With the partition of the island in 1974, the ethnic split became permanent. Greek Cypriots stay in the southern region, while Turkish Cypriots remain in

Pyla is one of Cyprus's few ethnically mixed towns. Ethnic Greeks and Turks lived together here for centuries and continued to do so after the island was partitioned in 1974. At left, the domes of Pyla's Orthodox Christian Church can be seen, while at right is the minaret (tower) of the Muslim mosque.

the north. With no contact between the groups, it is not unusual to find young people who have never talked to a Cypriot from a cultural group other than their own.

Today, Greek Cypriots make up about 85 percent of the population, while Turkish Cypriots make up about 12 percent. The remaining 3 percent are Maronites, Armenians, and Latins. Maronites are Christians whose ancestors came from Syria and Lebanon during the Byzantine period; most live in four villages in northwestern Cyprus. Most Armenians arrived after World War I, leaving Turkey to escape persecution. The Latins living on Cyprus today are descendants of the Lusignan and Venetian upper classes that ruled Cyprus from the thirteenth to sixteenth centuries. Most are of French or Italian heritage.

Land and Resources

Cyprus is not a large island, but it had many resources that attracted the interest of powerful empires. About 5,000 years ago, Cyprus became famous for its copper deposits. In fact, the word *copper* comes from the Greek name for Cyprus, which is Kupros.

Geography

Cyprus is a long island, stretching 140 miles (225 kilometers) from east to west. The narrow Karpas Peninsula that extends east toward Syria makes up about one-third of this length. At its widest point, Cyprus extends 60 miles (96 kilometers) from north to south. The island covers 3,571 square miles (9,250 square kilometers), making it the third largest island in the Mediterranean Sea after Sardinia and Sicily. Cyprus is roughly three-fourths the size of Connecticut.

Two major mountain ranges stretch across Cyprus. The forested Troodos Mountains cover much of the south and west. The highest point on Cyprus—Mount Olympus—is found in the Troodos Range. The Troodos Mountains are also home to rich copper deposits that have been mined since ancient days. The Kyrenia Range defines the northern coast. Although the limestone and marble peaks in this narrow ridge don't reach the heights of the Troodos Mountains, many visitors consider them more picturesque. One of the most distinctive peaks in the Kyrenia Range, Mount Pentadactylos, is named for the "five fingers" of white limestone that reach toward the sky.

Between the two mountain ranges lies the Mesaoria, a broad fertile plain. Once thickly forested, the Mesaoria is now the agricultural center of Cyprus. Grain crops such as wheat and barley are dependent upon seasonal rainfall, but most fruit and vegetable crops require irrigation.

Mesaoria is a Greek word that means "between the mountains."

Major Cities

Although Cyprus's coastal cities are now important centers for commerce and tourism, historically most Cypriots lived inland. The fertile soil of the Mesaoria enabled Cypriots to grow their own food and raise livestock, while the two mountain ranges provided some measure of safety from pirates and conquerors. In fact, the capital was moved inland to the city of Nicosia because of the constant Arab raids on coastal cities between the seventh and eleventh centuries.

Today, Nicosia is the largest city on Cyprus. The ancient section of the city still exists behind centuries-old stone walls. Narrow streets wind past museums, shops, tavernas (cafes), and medieval churches. Outside the walled city is Nicosia's modern commercial center. The city has been divided into Greek Cypriot and Turkish zones since 1974.

Limassol and Larnaca, the second and third largest cities, have developed into the principal southern ports. Both cities are popular tourist destinations, with beautiful beaches and ancient Greek and Roman ruins. On the northeast coast, Famagusta has become the chief port for the Turkish Cypriot region.

LIVING HISTORY

Cyprus has many historical sites that draw millions of tourists each year. Paphos is the legendary birthplace of Aphrodite, the Greek goddess of love. Its many magnificent ruins include long-buried mosaics, the Odeon Theater, and the Fontana Amarosa—the Fountain of Love, rumored to be the source of Aphrodite's love potion. Nearby, in the Troodos Mountains, are painted churches from the Byzantine era. On the eastern edge of the island in the city of Famagusta, a large stone castle, known as Othello's Tower, guards the harbor. It was the setting for part of William Shakespeare's tragedy, *Othello*.

In the Troodos Mountains of Cyprus, a spring snowfall covers the trees.

Climate

The climate on Cyprus is typical of the Mediterranean region. Long, hot summers are followed by mild, wet winters. The average rainfall varies significantly by region. The highest elevations of the Troodos Mountains record the heaviest annual rainfall, about 39 inches (1,000 millimeters). The northern coast averages about 16.7 inches (425 millimeters) per year, while the Mesaoria receives the least amount of rain—as little as 12 inches (300 millimeters). The amount of rain varies from year to year, however, and droughts occur frequently.

While summer temperatures throughout the island are uncomfortably hot in the lowlands, they often rise above 100° F (38° C) in the Mesaoria. Higher elevations provide a respite from the scorching heat. As a result, several villages in the Troodos Mountains have become popular tourist destinations in the summer months. During the winter, the same resorts offer skiing and other cold-weather sports.

Some regions of Cyprus are very dry and droughts occur often. A drought in the 1990s left some reservoirs at just 6 percent of their capacity. At this reservoir at the Lefka Dam, for instance, the water level should be where the line of trees starts on the hillside. The numbered markers show the normal volume of water.

Natural Resources

Rich deposits of minerals—including copper, gypsum, salt, and umber (a natural brown pigment used in paints)—established Cyprus as a prosperous trading center in ancient times. Although copper gave Cyprus its name and brought prosperity to the island, it is no longer of major commercial importance. Most of the copper mined today goes to crafts workers who create traditional and decorative copper items for the tourist trade.

In its early history, Cyprus was known for the thick forests of pine and cedar that covered the Mesaoria and Troodos regions. Over the centuries, builders harvested the trees in the Mesaoria to craft ships, churches, and homes. Peasant families cut trees for firewood, and their goats grazed on the young saplings. By the late 1800s, the central plain showed no sign of having once been a forest, and the mountain forests were threatened as well. Erosion was a serious problem.

Reforestation efforts, initiated by the British in 1878, continue today, primarily in the mountains and foothills where forest reserves can help prevent erosion and flooding. Shepherds, once able to let their flocks roam freely, faced tight restrictions in 1950 on where their animals could graze. They often opposed reforestation projects in the lowlands because they didn't want to give up any grazing lands. To ease these fears, forestry officials began planting grasses between the rows of eucalyptus trees. Once the trees were established, people were able to graze their sheep and cattle in the reforested areas.

The most important resource for an island—fresh water—is in short supply on Cyprus. There are no permanent rivers and very few freshwater lakes. Most water comes from underground aquifers and reservoirs designed to capture runoff during the rainy season. Water rationing is not uncommon, especially during the summer months. In recent years, the problem has been compounded by increased pollution. Saltwater has contaminated the main aquifer, and other freshwater sources are threatened by increasing industrial waste. In 1997, Cyprus built a desalination plant to convert saltwater into fresh water. More desalination plants are planned to provide a reliable supply of water.

Plants and Animals

Cypriots enjoy a rich diversity of plant life. Nearly 2,000 species and subspecies of plants are found on the island. Wildflowers bloom year-round, although they are most plentiful in the fall, winter, and spring. While trees no longer cover the central plains, a nature reserve was established in the Troodos region to protect the pine, cypress, and cedar trees of the Pathos Forest.

A rare type of wild sheep called the mouflon can only be found on Cyprus. Once near extinction due to deforestation and hunting, the mouflon has been protected as an endangered species since 1978. Today, mouflon sheep are found only in the Pathos Forest.

Millions of birds, including flamingos and wild ducks, stop at the salt lakes of Larnaca and Alrotiri as they migrate between Europe and Africa. Since medieval times, villagers have trapped the smaller birds, especially the endangered black caps, which many consider a delicacy. Though trapping is prohibited by law today, many Cypriots augment their income by trapping the birds and selling them to restaurants. Conservationists estimate that up to 2 million birds are trapped each year. With Cyprus's membership in the European Union being considered for the near future, the Cypriot government has strengthened its enforcement of the anti-trapping laws.

The biggest threat facing the plants and animals of Cyprus comes from changing land-use practices. As the Cypriot economy places greater dependence upon industry and tourism, habitats across the island are being damaged. Coastal and marine habitats are particularly threatened.

History

Ancient Days

No one is quite sure when the first humans arrived on Cyprus, but archaeological evidence shows that the island has been inhabited for nearly 8,000 years, since the Neolithic era (New Stone Age). The early settlers were most likely from nearby Asia Minor (present-day Turkey). When copper was discovered on the island around 3000 B.C.E., trading ships began visiting Cyprus regularly. Many of the ships brought settlers to mine the ore and transport it to the coast.

Trading expeditions by the Mycenaeans—ancient Greeks from the Peloponnese—became more frequent after 1400 B.C.E. A century passed before the Greeks began settling in Cyprus, but once the influx started, it was continuous. By 1000 B.C.E., the Greeks had spread their

IMPORTANT EVENTS IN CYPRUS'S HISTORY

5800 B.C.E. Human settlements are established.

3000 B.C.E. Copper is discovered; Cyprus becomes a trading center.

1400 B.C.E. Greek traders begin visiting Cyprus.

1184 B.C.E. Greek settlers begin arriving.

800 B.C.E. Phoenician settlers arrive in Kition.

708 B.C.E. Assyrians conquer Cyprus.

600 B.C.E. Egyptians conquer Cyprus.

525 B.C.E. Cyprus becomes part of the Persian Empire.

333 B.C.E. Alexander the Great conquers the Persian Empire; Cyprus is granted independence.

294 B.C.E. Ptolemy takes control of Cyprus.

58 B.C.E. Rome takes control of Cyprus.

647 C.E. Arab attacks against Cyprus begin, continuing for over 300 years.

1184 Byzantine governor Isaac Comnenos declares himself king of Cyprus.

1191 King Richard I (Lionheart) of England captures Cyprus.

1260 Pope Alexander IV declares the Roman Catholic Church to be the official church of Cyprus.

1291 Cyprus becomes a base of operations for Christians fighting against Muslims during the Crusades.

1468 Cyprus aligns itself with Venice.

1489 Venice officially annexes Cyprus.

1570 Ottoman Turks invade Cyprus and take control of the island.

1850 Greek Cypriots begin pushing for enosis, or unification with Greece.

1878 The Ottoman Empire cedes control of Cyprus to Britain.

1914 Britain annexes Cyprus when the Ottoman Empire joins forces with Germany during World War I.

1925 Cyprus becomes a British colony.

1940 Cypriot volunteers join British forces in World War II.

1941 Communists form Progressive Party of the Working People (Cypriot acronym AKEL) in Cyprus.

1950 Cypriot vote on proposal of enosis receives 96 percent approval.

1954 United Nations refuses to consider self-determination for Cyprus; riots break out; the National Organization of Cypriot Fighters (Cypriot acronym EOKA) forms.

1955 British, Turkish, and Greek leaders discuss the future of Cyprus.

1956 Makarios and other church leaders are exiled.

1959 Greece and Turkey accept compromise agreement supporting independence for Cyprus.

1960 The Republic of Cyprus officially gains independence on August 16; Makarios is elected president.

1963 Turkish Cypriots cease participation in government; fighting between Turkish and Greek Cypriots breaks out.

1964 UN stations peacekeeping forces on Cyprus.

1967 Greece and Turkey near war over events on Cyprus; after negotiations, Greece withdraws forces and Turkey disbands its invasion forces.

1968 Makarios overwhelmingly wins reelection as president.

1971 Backed by the Greek government, EOKA is rebuilt as EOKA-B, and launches guerrilla attacks against the Makarios government.

1974 Cypriot National Guard overthrows the government; Turkish forces invade Cyprus and seize control of nearly 40 percent of the country.

1983 Turkish Cypriots create the independent Turkish Republic of Northern Cyprus.

1999 UN initiates reunification talks; European Union considers Cyprus for membership in 2004.

2003 Reunification talks fail; the Republic of Cyprus prepares to enter the European Union by itself.

language, religion, and culture throughout Cyprus. They identified a spot near Paphos on the southwest coast as the birthplace of Aphrodite, Greek goddess of love and beauty. The temple that was built nearby to honor her attracted worshipers throughout the region.

As the first millennium B.C.E. began, Cyprus was organized into seven independent city-kingdoms with kings who served as both political and religious leaders. About 800 B.C.E., Phoenician settlers began arriving in Cyprus, especially around Kition (present-day Larnaca). A century later, Sargon II, the king of Assyria, conquered Cyprus. The Cypriot kings were allowed quite a bit of independence, however, and many became wealthy under Assyrian rule. Three more Cypriot kingdoms were established, one of which was Phoenician.

In a ruined basilica, or church, in Salamis, workers repair part of a tiled floor after archaeologists finished looking for artifacts. During the time that Cyprus was part of the Persian Empire, Salamis became its most important city-kingdom.

By the end of the seventh century B.C.E., the decline of the Assyrian Empire left Cyprus vulnerable to attacks by Egypt, which sent warships to conquer the Cypriots. Once again, the ruling empire was more interested in the copper and timber that Cyprus offered than in controlling its people, so the Cypriot kings retained much of their power.

Cyprus was incorporated into the Persian Empire after the Persians conquered the Egyptians in 525 B.C.E. For the next two centuries, Persian rulers controlled Cyprus. Salamis, on the east coast of Cyprus, became the most important city-kingdom during this period. Several of its kings launched revolts against the Persians, although none were successful. The predominantly Greek culture continued to flourish on the island. By 374 B.C.E., the Greek alphabet was in use on Cyprus, and Greek artists and scholars were invited to the courts of some Cypriot kings.

Cyprus enjoyed a brief period of independence following Alexander the Great's defeat of Persia in 333 B.C.E. Following Alexander's death ten years later, Cyprus was caught in a tug-of-war between his heirs. Ptolemy, a former general of Alexander's and governor of Egypt, eventually won control of Cyprus in 294 B.C.E. Over the next two centuries, Ptolemy and his heirs dismantled the Cypriot kingdoms and established a central government.

When the Romans *annexed* Cyprus in 58 B.C.E., they designated the city of Paphos as their government seat. The city of Salamis in the east remained the cultural, educational, and commercial center of the island. Cyprus prospered as the Romans constructed roads, harbors, and public buildings.

The arrival of Christianity in Cyprus occurred during Roman rule. Because of its location, Cyprus was one of the early destinations of Christian missionaries. In 45 C.E., the apostles Paul and Barnabas

THE HIDDEN CITY

Salamis, once the most important city on Cyprus, suffered two devastating earthquakes during Roman rule. The city was rebuilt each time and became the capital once again under Byzantine rule. In the seventh century, Arabs invaded Cyprus and massacred most of the citizens of Salamis (then called Constantia). Those who survived fled to other cities. Salamis was eventually covered by drifting sand. Archaeologists began excavating the site in 1952, uncovering coins from the fourth century B.C.E. as well as extensive Roman ruins and a Byzantine-era basilica (church). Today, the site draws tourists from around the world.

arrived in Salamis, Barnabas's hometown, and began preaching. The Roman governor soon converted to Christianity, making Cyprus the first region within the empire to be ruled by a Christian.

The Byzantine Empire

The Roman Empire was divided into two regions in 285 C.E. The western half of the empire spoke Latin, while the eastern half spoke Greek. In 330, Constantine the Great became the emperor of the Eastern Empire and the first Christian Roman emperor. He established his capital in the city of Byzantium (bih-ZAN-shee-um), which he renamed Constantinople (present-day Istanbul). The Eastern Empire became known as the Byzantine (BIH-zuhn-teen) Empire, or Byzantium. Cyprus fell within the jurisdiction of the Byzantine Empire and remained under its rule for the next 800 years.

Christianity was well established on Cyprus by the time Constantine the Great came to power. In 431, the Church of Cyprus was recognized as an independent church, able to elect its own bishops and archbishops. Church leaders grew more powerful and were closely affiliated with the government.

The early centuries of Byzantine rule were relatively peaceful and prosperous. The peasants lost their freedom, however, when Constantine declared all tenant farmers to be serfs. They were not allowed to leave the land where they were born; runaways could be severely punished.

AT THIS POINT IN TIME

In 1096 C.E., a group of volunteer Christian soldiers set out from Western Europe. Their goal, which they accomplished in 1099, was to travel to the city of Jerusalem and wrest control of it from the Muslims. This religious war became known as the First Crusade.

The Second Crusade was launched in 1144, after Muslims recaptured some of the Christian territory in the Holy Land. It was not successful; many Western soldiers died in the fighting. The Muslims, led by Saladin, took control of Jerusalem once again in 1187.

The goal of the Crusades, which were mounted by Christian armies that originated in Western Europe, was to gain control of Jerusalem, a city also considered holy by Muslims.

Arab attacks, beginning in 647, destroyed the peace and signaled the start of 300 years of conflict. Some raids were quick strikes, but others were full-blown assaults on major cities. The Arab invaders massacred thousands of Cypriots and took thousands more into slavery. Countless treasures were looted or destroyed. The population centers shifted inland as Cypriots fled the great devastation caused by the Arab attacks. Nicosia, located in the Mesaoria, became the capital city of Cyprus during this time.

In the late twelfth century, a Byzantine governor—Isaac Comnenos—declared himself king of Cyprus. A harsh and cruel man, Comnenos made a mistake in 1191 that cost him the control of Cyprus: he looted some ships that had been damaged in a storm. One of the ships belonged to the fiancée of King Richard I of England, who was one of the leaders of the Third Crusade. Furious at the treatment his fiancée had received, Richard attacked Comnenos and won control of Cyprus.

Faced with the reality of ruling over a faraway island, Richard soon sold Cyprus to the Knights Templars, professional soldiers who supported the Crusades. In 1192, they turned control of the island over to Guy de Lusignan, former Christian king of Jerusalem. This marked the end of 800 years of Byzantine rule in Cyprus.

The Lusignan Dynasty

Cypriots were not pleased with the changes that were taking place on their island. Although the new ruler was Christian, as were most Cypriots, de Lusignan was Roman Catholic and the Cypriots were Greek Orthodox. Within a few years, Catholic churches had been established and were demanding tithes (a tax of 10 percent used to support the church). Land was seized from the Greek Cypriots and given to members of the noble class, all foreigners. In 1260, the pope announced that the Roman Catholic Church was the official church of Cyprus. Most Greek Cypriots ignored this declaration and continued to follow their Greek Orthodox traditions.

As the only Christian country in the region, Cyprus became an important base for Europeans. Some used Cyprus as a launch for their continued Crusades against the Muslims, while others used it as a base for the silk and spice trade with Asia. It was a very prosperous time for the upper-class families and the Catholic Church. They used their wealth to build beautiful castles and spectacular cathedrals. Heavily fortified cities, often surrounded by thick stone walls, protected Cypriots from attacks by neighboring countries.

In 1468, the republic of Venice (in present-day Italy) gained control of Cyprus and ruled for the next eighty-two years. These years were marked by increasingly frequent attacks by the Ottomans (leaders of the early Turkish empire). At first, the Ottomans led raids on coastal cities, but in 1570 the raids escalated into an invasion. The city of Nicosia was besieged, and over 20,000 Greek Cypriots were slaughtered. Within a year, the Ottomans controlled all of Cyprus.

The Ottoman Period

The Ottomans made two immediate changes that had long-lasting effects. First, they implemented their system of ruling through *millets,* or religious communities. This strengthened the Greek Orthodox community, establishing a precedent for combined religious and political leadership. Second, the Ottomans gave much of the land they seized from the upper classes to Ottoman soldiers and settlers, creating a permanent Turkish community on Cyprus.

As non-Muslims, Greek Cypriots were taxed heavily, but there was no pressure to convert to Islam. In fact, the Ottomans allowed the Church of Cyprus to regain its former prominence. Content with collecting taxes, the Ottoman rulers let the infrastructure of Cyprus—the roads, bridges, harbors, and forts—all fall into disrepair. The poverty-stricken peasants suffered through droughts and famine with no assistance from the Ottoman government. From time to time, Greek Cypriots led rebellions against the Ottoman government, but none were successful. By the mid-nineteenth century, most Greek Cypriots had embraced the dream of enosis, or union with Greece.

British Rule

In the nineteenth century, the Ottoman Empire felt increasingly threatened by Russian encroachment on its territory. At the same time, Western European nations worried about Russia expanding its borders. In 1878, the Ottomans agreed to place Cyprus under British control in return for military protection if Russia attacked. Britain was to make an annual payment to the Ottomans, a technicality designed to show that Cyprus remained an Ottoman possession.

When the Ottomans joined forces with Germany—an enemy of Britain—at the beginning of World War I (1914–1918), Britain terminated its agreement with the Ottomans and annexed Cyprus. It became a British colony in 1925.

Under British rule, the infrastructure was modernized. Dams were built to capture rainwater. Irrigation systems, roads, and railways were constructed. A reforestation program was established to control erosion and water capture. The school system was expanded, making at least a primary education available to all children. Health care facilities were built, and eventually diseases such as malaria were eliminated.

In this illustration, the British flag is raised in Cyprus after Britain gained control of the island in 1878. Technically, Cyprus was still the property of the Ottoman Empire, but that was to change in 1925 when it became a British colony after the Ottomans allied themselves with Germany, Britain's enemy, in World War I.

These improvements came at a great cost, however. The Cypriots were heavily taxed, at first to cover the annual payment to Turkey and later to cover defense. In 1931, the British proposed an increase in taxes in spite of the worldwide economic depression. Riots broke out across Cyprus as people protested the proposal. In response, the British severely restricted the rights of the Cypriots, suspending the constitution and allowing the governor dictatorial powers. Leaders of the riots—including two Greek Orthodox bishops—were *exiled*, political parties were outlawed, and newspapers were censored. In addition, schools were not allowed to teach Greek or Turkish history. Greek Cypriots were particularly outraged when Britain passed a series of laws placing the Church of Cyprus under the control of the British government.

In 1941, Britain relaxed some of the restrictions against political activity. Communists quickly formed the Progressive Party of the Working People (acronym AKEL). Within five years, AKEL-sponsored mayoral candidates had won election in three major cities—Limassol, Famagusta, and Nicosia.

In 1946, the British announced plans to form a Consultative Assembly to discuss a new constitution. They also repealed the religious laws and allowed those who had been exiled in 1931 to return home. The announcements were met with anger from Greek Cypriots who had expected some mention of enosis. To Britain's dismay, most Greek Cypriots refused to participate in the Consultative Assembly unless enosis was a possibility. Turkish Cypriots and AKEL leaders attended the assembly meeting, but when the British refused to consider Cypriot self-government, AKEL joined the remaining Greek Cypriots in opposing continued British rule.

In 1948, the push for enosis gained new momentum when the young bishop of Kition, Makarios (muh-KAR-ee-us), became political adviser to the archbishop. When Makarios set up a referendum in which Greek Cypriots could vote on the issue of enosis in 1950, an astonishing 96 percent voted in favor of union with Greece. The overwhelmingly positive results were presented to Greece and the UN in hope of building support for self-determination—the Cypriots' right to choose how and by whom they would be governed. Britain maintained that, as a crown colony, the governance of Cyprus was Britain's own internal concern. Britain opposed enosis, at least in part because the Turkish

Cypriots spoke out so strongly against it. Conflict between Greece and Turkey would be a distinct possibility if Cyprus became part of Greece.

As the Greek Cypriot call for self-determination grew louder, Turkish Cypriots began pushing for *partition*. As a minority group under British rule, the Turkish Cypriot interests were protected. If Cyprus became part of Greece, however, the Turkish Cypriots would have little voice in government. They felt that their interests would be best protected if they had their own, separate government and country.

Makarios, the bishop of Kition, was instrumental in the push for the union of Cyprus with Greece, setting up an election in 1950 that showed the Cypriots' overwhelming support of it, too. Makarios was later exiled along with other church leaders for encouraging strikes and violence against the British.

In 1954, however, the UN refused to make a recommendation allowing Cyprus self-determination. A general strike was called, and rioting was widespread. A group of Greek Cypriots, led by George Grivas, formed the National Organization of Cypriot Fighters (Greek acronym EOKA). In 1955, EOKA launched a series of *guerrilla* attacks against the British government, including the police and the military. British leaders declared a state of emergency. Public meetings and strikes were banned, and carrying a weapon became a crime punishable by death. Archbishop Makarios and several other church leaders were exiled in 1956 for their role in encouraging strikes and violence. Grivas became the unofficial leader of the Greek Cypriots, and EOKA increased its violent attacks. Turkish Cypriots formed a guerrilla group of their own, the Turkish Resistance Organization. Hostilities between the Greek and Turkish Cypriot communities became more common and more violent.

Finally, in 1958, representatives from Greece and Turkey met with British leaders to discuss the Cyprus problem. They finally agreed that independence was the best solution. Britain signed a treaty with Greece and Turkey that guaranteed Cyprus's independence. The treaty stated that any of the three countries could send troops to Cyprus if it was in danger of losing its independence to another country.

Independence

Independence was granted on August 16, 1960. Since Greek Cypriots make up about 85 percent of the population, the new constitution tried to provide an equitable representation for Turkish Cypriots. Under the assumption that Greek Cypriots would always elect one of their candidates for president, the office of vice president was reserved for a Turkish Cypriot. All government groups, from the legislature to the military, were required to reflect the proportion of Greek and Turkish Cypriots. Laws could not be passed without the approval of more than half of the members of both the Greek and Turkish Cypriot delegations.

The dividing line in Nicosia is called the "Green Line" because the first person to mark it on a map used a green marker.

The new political structure was too complicated to work well, especially when the two groups did not trust each other. In 1963, following an outbreak of violent fighting between the Greek and Turkish Cypriot communities, the Turkish vice president and members of the

House of Representatives stopped participating in the government. As the violence continued, Turkish Cypriots began migrating from rural areas into enclaves—communities that are completely composed of one ethnic group—for security. Many relocated into the northern section of Nicosia.

In 1964, the UN sent a peacekeeping force to Cyprus. The Greek Cypriot legislature established the National Guard in an attempt to control the growing number of undisciplined militia groups. Makarios appointed EOKA leader George Grivas to command the National Guard. Turkey, claiming that troops from Greece were also being included in the National Guard, began planning an invasion of Cyprus. The invasion was called off after the United States intervened with a warning, however.

The 1958 treaty signed by Great Britain, Greece, and Turkey that guaranteed Cyprus's independence was sealed with the three-way handshake of (left to right) Prime Minister Harold Macmillan of Great Britain, Foreign Minister Fatin Zorlu of Turkey, and President Constantine Caramanlis of Greece.

The situation continued to deteriorate, and in 1967, twenty-six Turkish Cypriots were killed by National Guard troops patrolling the ethnic enclaves. Turkey threatened to send thousands of troops to Cyprus to protect the Turkish Cypriots unless certain demands were met, including the exile of Grivas from Cyprus, the dismantling of the National Guard, and the removal of Greek troops from the island. The threat of war between Turkey and Greece, with Cyprus in the middle, again hung over the region until late 1967, when Greece agreed to withdraw its troops from Cyprus. Grivas left the island as well, but the National Guard remained firmly entrenched.

A Divided Country

At the end of 1967, Turkish Cypriot leaders established a provisional administration to govern their community. They did not claim that they were a new government, but most observers saw the move as the first step toward partition. The Greek Cypriots held the presidential election in 1968. Makarios won reelection with 96 percent of the vote.

The UN led peace talks throughout the early 1970s, but little progress was made. Grivas secretly returned to the island in 1971 and organized a new guerrilla group called EOKA-B, funded by the Greek government. Its main goal was the overthrow of Makarios, an objective that was shared by the officers of the Cypriot National Guard—many of whom had served in the Greek military.

The Turkish Invasion

In the early months of 1974, the plot by Greece and the National Guard to overthrow Makarios was discovered by Cypriot intelligence. When Makarios exposed the plot in July, the Greek government gave the order for the National Guard to take control of Cyprus. Barely escaping being killed during the *coup*, Makarios fled to London.

To stop Greece from completely controlling Cyprus, Turkey sent 40,000 troops to the island. Thousands of Greek Cypriots fled southward to escape attack. Likewise, Turkish Cypriots fled to the north. By August 16, Turkey controlled the northern 37 percent of Cyprus—from Morphou Bay to Famagusta. The division took place along what was called the "Atilla Line."

The Greek coup and Turkish invasion caused a great deal of human suffering and loss. Thousands were killed in the fighting. About one-third of both the Greek Cypriot and Turkish Cypriot communities became refugees in their own country. With the island divided, the economy was shattered—both ethnic regions prohibited movement of people or products across the Atilla Line.

Given the devastation that occurred in 1974, the recovery took place relatively quickly—in just a few years. Housing was hastily constructed for the refugees, and schools were expanded. The economy in both regions shifted to place more emphasis on tourism and industry. The Turkish Cypriots had a greater struggle to rebuild, because the Republic of Cyprus had placed a trade embargo on the region. However, they received aid from Turkey, which helped them develop a decent standard of living.

Two separate governments ruled over the island. The Republic of Cyprus continued under Greek Cypriot control. Makarios returned to Cyprus in late 1974 and served as president until his death in 1977. The current president, Tassos Papadopoulos, was elected in 2003. The Turkish Cypriots, declaring their intention to govern themselves,

A military parade in the Turkish part of Nicosia, Cyprus, marks the anniversary of Turkey's invasion of Cyprus, by which Turkey maintained its control of a portion of the island. For Turkish Cypriots, the occasion is a time of pride. For Greek Cypriots to the south, however, it is a sad reminder of the suffering that resulted.

established the Turkish Federated State of Cyprus in 1975. In 1983, after negotiations for reuniting Cyprus had failed, Turkish Cypriots created the independent Turkish Republic of Northern Cyprus (TRNC), recognized only by Turkey. (The Greek Cypriot government refers to the north as "the occupied territory.") Rauf Denktas, a long-time leader of the Turkish Cypriot community, was elected president of the TRNC in 1983—a post he still holds today.

Cyprus Today

Since 1974, Cypriots have lived in a divided country. A UN peacekeeping force remains on the island, guarding the buffer zone along the Atilla Line. Although many peace talks have been held over the past three decades, little progress was made toward reunification. In 1998, when the European Union (EU) began to plan for its 2004 expansion, Cyprus was one of the countries under consideration for

THE EUROPEAN UNION

The European Union began in 1950 as a coalition of six nations—France, Belgium, the Federal Republic of Germany, Italy, Luxembourg, and the Netherlands—that sought to unify European coal and steel production in order to speed economic recovery after World War II (1939–1945). The success of this venture resulted in the founding of the European Economic Community (EEC) in 1955. The EEC created a market in which member countries' citizens, goods, money, and services could move freely. In 1993, a new treaty transformed the EEC into the European Union (EU). Plans were made to develop a common currency—the euro—to simplify trade and strengthen European monetary policy. In addition, the 1993 treaty made it easier for participating countries to cooperate in legal and police matters.

To become a member of the European Union, a country must have a stable democratic government, a good human rights record, a market economy, and solid economic policies. Today, fifteen countries belong to the European Union, although only twelve have adopted the euro since its introduction in 2002.

Turkish Cypriots demonstrate in favor of a unified Cyprus for inclusion in the European Union, in support of a plan backed by the United Nations.

membership. The UN reopened negotiations with Greek and Turkish Cypriot leaders, hoping the island could be reunited before the EU treaty was signed in April 2003. Last-ditch efforts failed, however, and Cyprus remains divided. The Greek Cypriot-controlled Republic of Cyprus will become a member of the European Union in 2004.

Economy

Cyprus's economy boomed during and after World War II due to the rise in construction to accommodate the British military, which was using the island as a base of operation. Cyprus thrived as a commercial center after the war. However, the Turkish invasion of 1974 and subsequent partition caused an economic setback.

Since 1974, the Republic of Cyprus has reestablished a prosperous, fast-growing economy based primarily on tourism, real estate, manufacturing, and shipping. The living standard of Greek Cypriots has increased steadily. The economic future of the Republic of Cyprus, set to enter the European Union in 2004, looks promising.

Although negatively affected by political events early in the twenty-first century, tourism is still a major industry in Cyprus, as this crowded beach in Ayia Napa demonstrates. The island's Mediterranean location, natural beauty, and history all contribute to its attraction.

The Turkish Republic of Northern Cyprus has had a more difficult time regaining its economic footing. Because the international community does not recognize it as an independent country, the TRNC is not eligible for international aid and loans and is heavily dependent on economic aid from Turkey. Foreign businesses are reluctant to invest in the TRNC or to relocate there because of its uncertain status. In addition, water shortages have plagued the region, requiring the construction of expensive desalination plants. The economy is stagnant, with growth estimated at 1 percent, while inflation rates have reached upwards of 50 percent. The TRNC's refusal to consider reunification made it ineligible to join the European Union, a prospect that could have brightened its gloomy economic future.

Business and Industry

In recent years, both the Republic of Cyprus and the TRNC have capitalized on Cyprus's Mediterranean location, natural beauty, and ancient history to develop a strong tourism industry. Tourism is

Mining is another industry that contributes to the economy of Cyprus. Copper from this mine, which is owned by an American company, is exported to Europe.

vulnerable to outside influences, however. Violence and civil unrest in the Middle East, along with terrorist attacks in the United States and elsewhere, have negatively affected Cyprus's tourism industry in recent years, as has the slowing economy in Western Europe.

Much of the best agricultural land is in the north, where the export of citrus fruit and potatoes is responsible for about 8 percent of the TRNC's income. The textile industry is also very important to the Turkish Cypriot economy. While the Greek Cypriots don't rely as heavily on agriculture, they do export a significant amount of citrus fruit, potatoes, grapes, and wine. The production of clothing, shoes, and cement also contributes to the Greek Cypriot economy.

One unexpected consequence of the Turkish invasion was the effect that it had on land prices in the south. When thousands of Greek Cypriots relocated from northern Cyprus to the south in 1974, land became scarce. As the tourism industry grew, the land increased in value. Many families today are quite wealthy because of this phenomenon.

Media and Communications

Both regions of Cyprus have excellent communications systems. Traditional telephone service is reliable and up-to-date, and cellular phones are widely used. Television arrived in Cyprus in 1956. Today, the Greek and Turkish Cypriot broadcasters host four stations apiece. Internet use is growing rapidly, with six providers on the island serving an estimated 150,000 users.

Religion and Beliefs

Religion has played a vital role in Cyprus's history. The Church of Cyprus, one of the earliest Christian churches to be established in the eastern Roman (Byzantine) Empire, has always had influence on the politics of the island. Islam was introduced under Ottoman rule when Turkish settlers arrived in Cyprus. Today, 78 percent of Cyprus's population is Eastern (Greek) Orthodox Christian. Islam, practiced by 18 percent of the population, is the predominant religion in the TRNC. Small groups of Maronite and Armenian Christians keep their religious traditions alive on Cyprus as well.

Eastern Orthodox

In the early centuries of Christianity, there were no denominations such as there are today. Instead, each church took the name of the community in which it was established. As the Roman Empire grew, Rome became the center of the Christian church in the West and Constantinople (present-day Istanbul, Turkey) became the center of churches in the East.

Leaders of the church called bishops met periodically to discuss and define church doctrine (beliefs). Over the centuries, differences emerged. When the Roman pope claimed divine authority to rule all churches and establish doctrine, the bishops of the Eastern Church protested. They believed that the pope and his eastern counterpart—the patriarch of Constantinople—were equal in stature to other bishops. They also believed that churches should govern themselves locally. In 1054, the Christian Church split into two churches—the Roman Catholic Church in the West and the Eastern Orthodox Church.

Orthodox church leaders from several nations gathered in Jerusalem in January 2000 to celebrate the new millennium. It had been nearly four centuries since the last such gathering of Orthodox leaders. In this picture are leaders from Greece, Romania, Serbia, Bulgaria, and Russia.

Christianity was introduced on Cyprus in 45 C.E., and the Church of Cyprus was established soon after that. As a church in the Eastern (Byzantine) Empire, the Church of Cyprus followed the Greek Orthodox rites after the split in 1054. The church is considered an independent church, however, which means that all decisions concerning the church are made at a local level rather than by a church hierarchy.

Like other Christians, Orthodox Cypriots believe that God exists in the form of the Father, Son, and Holy Spirit. Sacraments (religious ceremonies) such as baptism, confirmation, communion, and matrimony are celebrated as gifts from God that provide the grace and strength needed to live a holy life. Icons—holy paintings of God, saints, and angels that are blessed by the church—are an important part of the Orthodox tradition. Icons are found in many Orthodox homes as well as churches. Orthodox Christians believe that sacred contemplation of an icon can mystically bring a believer into the presence of the one depicted in the icon.

Church services are highly ritualized, with singing and incense. Traditionally, rural villagers attend services more frequently than educated Cypriots in urban areas, and women are more likely to be active in the church than men. For many Greek Cypriots, religious activities center on rituals at home, veneration (adoration) of icons, and observance of feast days.

Many Orthodox churches, monasteries, and convents on Cyprus are recognized throughout the world for their historical value as well as their beauty. Of the monasteries, the most famous is the Kykko Monastery in the Troodos region, but the Stavrovouni Monastery near Larnaca also draws many visitors. Also in the Troodos region are nine painted churches from the Byzantine era, some of which date back to the eleventh century. With intricately detailed murals painted on the interior walls, the churches were built within an outer stone building to protect them from harsh winters. In 1985, the United Nations Educational, Scientific and Cultural Organization (UNESCO) recognized the churches as a World Heritage site, a status that should help to protect them for the future.

Christianity

Christianity, which grew out of the Jewish religion and culture, began about 2,000 years ago in the land of Judea, now known as the nation of Israel. The first Christians were Jews who maintained Jewish religious practices, scripture, and culture, but who also believed that Jesus Christ was the Messiah (savior) sent by God to save Israel and all humanity from sin and death. Christians believe in one god, the same god worshiped by Jews and Muslims.

Basic Beliefs

Three basic beliefs are the foundation of the Christian religion:

• There is one God who exists as the Trinity—the Father, Son, and Holy Spirit—in one divine person. The Father is the God of the Old Testament who sent Jesus Christ to redeem the world. The Son is Jesus Christ, God's son, who came to earth as a man. The Holy Spirit, sometimes referred to as the Holy Ghost, is the presence of God as experienced by human beings.

• Jesus Christ was resurrected three days after his death and then ascended into heaven to live with God.

• People can be saved from sin and granted salvation and eternal life with God through their faith in Jesus Christ.

Sunday is the Christian holy day, chosen because it was on a Sunday that Christ was resurrected. Worship services generally include prayers, Bible readings, singing, and a sermon. Holy Communion symbolizes Jesus' sacrifice for humanity. According to Christian tradition, as Christians eat a piece of bread and sip wine or grape juice during Communion, they receive forgiveness for their sins. Some denominations celebrate Holy Communion during every church service, others once a month or less.

Forms of Christianity

Soon after Jesus' death and resurrection, his disciples (followers) spread Jesus' teachings throughout the Roman Empire. The new religion became known as Christianity, and followers were called Christians. By the end of the fourth century, Christianity was declared the official religion of the Roman Empire. When the empire was split into the Byzantine Empire in the East and the Roman Empire in the West, the practices of the Christian churches in these two regions began to diverge. The Western church, led by the pope in Rome, became known as the Roman Catholic Church, while the church in the Byzantine Empire—the Eastern Orthodox Church—was led by the patriarch in Constantinople.

In 1517, the German monk Martin Luther began a movement called the Reformation. Luther disagreed with the Roman Catholic Church over the concept of salvation and wanted to change church teachings. This conflict split the Western church into the Roman Catholic Church and a new Protestant church. The Protestant church formed many new churches–often called denominations—some of which we know today as Baptists, Methodists, Lutherans, Presbyterians, Episcopalians, and Congregationalists. Today, there are over 30,000 separate Christian denominations worldwide.

This researcher displays a Bible, printed in 1519, that belonged to Martin Luther, the founder of the Protestant church. The Bible contains Luther's own handwritten notes.

Sources of Christian Teachings and Beliefs

The Christian holy book is the Bible, which consists of two parts, the Old Testament and the New Testament, although different denominations have selected different parts to include in both. The Old Testament is based on the Jewish Bible. Some Bibles—including those used by the Roman Catholic Church and the Eastern Orthodox Church—include Jewish texts known as the Apocrypha in the Old Testament as well.

The first four books of the New Testament are known as the Gospels, or the good news. They were written by four of Jesus' disciples, who relate Jesus' teachings, describe the miracles he performed, and recount the circumstances of his crucifixion and resurrection. Other books in the New Testament include letters written by the apostles Paul and John to early Christian communities; the Book of Acts, which describes the early days of Christianity; and the Book of Revelation,

Called the Gutenberg Bible after Johannes Gutenberg, the inventor of the first printing press, is perhaps the most famous copy of the Bible, the Christian holy book. It was made in the 1450s and was one of the first books to be printed by a machine instead of copied by hand.

a collection of prophecies about the second coming of Christ and the end of the world.

While the stories contained in the Bible are important to all Christians, not everyone interprets them in the same way. Conservative Christians believe that the Bible is the literal, unerring word of God, while other Christians believe that many stories in the Bible are metaphors that illustrate the right way to live.

Major Holidays

All Christians celebrate three major holiday seasons: Easter, Pentecost, and Christmas. In addition, the Catholic and Orthodox churches observe holidays associated with the saints of the church and with people in Jesus' life, such as his parents, Joseph and Mary.

Easter Season Easter, which celebrates the resurrection of Jesus Christ, is the most important day in the Christian church calendar. The Easter season begins with Lent, a forty-day period in which Christians prepare spiritually for Easter. Some Christians avoid meat or fast on certain days during Lent. The week before Easter is called Holy Week. It begins with Palm Sunday, which marks Jesus' entry into Jerusalem. Maundy Thursday, the commemoration of the Lord's Supper, and Good Friday, recalling Jesus' punishment by crucifixion, are both solemn holy days. Christians rejoice on Easter Sunday, remembering Christ's resurrection on the third day after his death. Brightly decorated eggs, symbolic of new life, are often part of Easter celebrations.

Pentecost Pentecost, fifty days after Easter, commemorates the Holy Spirit descending upon early Christians. Over time, the entire period between Easter and Pentecost became known as Pentecost. This season is a joyful time, celebrating Jesus' resurrection and the gift of salvation. The Day of Ascension, honoring the ascension of Jesus into heaven, occurs during the season of Pentecost, on the fortieth day after Easter.

Christmas Season Advent, beginning on the fourth Sunday before Christmas, marks the start of the Christian year as well as the Christmas season. During Advent, Christians prepare to celebrate the birth of Jesus Christ and to welcome the return of Christ. Members of Eastern Orthodox churches often take part in fasts to show their remorse for sinning, while other Christians focus on prayer and the anticipation that the season evokes.

Christmas is celebrated on December 25 in the Western churches. In many Eastern churches, which follow a different calendar, Christmas falls in January.

Epiphany, sometimes called Three Kings' Day, marks the end of the Christmas season. Observed on January 6 in most traditions, Epiphany commemorates the coming of the three wise men, or magi, who revealed baby Jesus as the Messiah. In between Christmas and Epiphany are the Twelve Days of Christmas.

Christianity Today

Today, Christianity is one of the three major religions of the world. (Judiasm and Islam are the other two.) With almost 2 billion followers, Christians make up approximately one-third of the world's population. Christianity is growing most rapidly in South America, South Africa, and parts of Asia.

Three men, dressed as the magi, ride in a parade to celebrate Three Kings' Day, or Epiphany. Marking the end of the Christian Christmas season, Epiphany is celebrated on the sixth of January each year.

Islam

Islam is the major religion in northern Cyprus, although the people living in the TRNC are free to worship as they please. Most Turkish Cypriots are Sunni Muslims and use an Arabic translation of the Qur'an.

Muslims follow the teachings of the Prophet Mohammad, who established Islam in the seventh century. They believe in one god—Allah—who revealed the Qur'an to Mohammad, the last in a series of prophets that includes Abraham and Jesus. Devout Muslims observe the five pillars of Islam: professing that "there is no God but God and Mohammad is his messenger," praying five times daily, fasting during the holy month of Ramadan, giving alms (charity) to the poor, and making a pilgrimage to Mecca, the birthplace of Mohammad. (To learn more about Islam, see page ix in the introduction to this volume.)

The traditional spiritual leader of the Turkish Cypriots is the *mufti*. Over the years, however, Turkish Cypriot society has become more secular—that is, less bound by religion. Today, the mufti is elected by Turkish Cypriots but has little control over laws, marriage, or education. Turkish Cypriots consider religion a personal matter. While many Muslims on Cyprus fast during Ramadan and observe holy days, most do not strictly observe Islamic principles such as abstaining from alcohol throughout the rest of the year. However, some foreign Islamic groups, including those from Saudi Arabia and Libya, are providing funds for new mosques and religious schools in northern Cyprus. They advocate a stronger role for Islam in the TRNC government.

Other Religions

The Maronite Church was established in Lebanon in the fifth century. It is affiliated with the Roman Catholic Church but conducts services using the ancient Syrian liturgy rather than a Latin one. Most Cypriot Maronites live in the village of Kormacit (Kormatiki) in northwestern Cyprus, where their ancestors settled about 1,200 years ago.

The Armenian Apostolic Orthodox Church is an independent Christian church. It was established in the first century C.E. when two apostles, Bartholomew and Thaddeus, introduced Christianity to Armenia. It became the official religion of Armenia in 301 C.E. The Armenian Church is led by the *catholicos*, or universal bishop. Although there has been an Armenian presence on Cyprus for centuries, most of the Armenians presently living on Cyprus are the descendants of refugees who arrived in the early twentieth century after the forced deportation and massacre of Armenians by the Ottomans. After the 1974 partition, most Armenian Cypriots settled in Nicosia, Larnaca, and Limassol.

Everyday Life

Both Turkish and Greek Cypriots have seen major changes in their lives over the past three decades. The civil unrest and push for enosis that resulted in the Turkish invasion of 1974 forced more people into urban areas, disrupting an agricultural lifestyle that had lasted for centuries. However, the basic values and traditions of the Greek and Turkish Cypriots remain strong today.

Over the last few decades, many Turkish and Greek Cypriots have moved to cities; fewer families live a traditional agricultural lifestyle.

Family Life

Many aspects of family life changed following the Turkish invasion. Many rural Greek Cypriot families lost their homes in the north and had to move to cities in the south. This opened up their access to education, which had a modernizing effect on the culture. Within this new environment, the Church of Cyprus lost some of its influence, which resulted in the more open, secular society seen today. Marriage and family ties remained strong, however, thanks to a tradition of identifying oneself primarily as part of a family rather than as an inhabitant of a particular location.

As more women were included in the education system, their roles slowly changed. Many began working outside the home. As men and women interacted more in schools, the workplace, and society, fewer marriages were arranged by matchmakers.

> ### Did You Know?
> Before World War II, a bridegroom was expected to provide a home as part of the wedding dowry, while the bride's family provided the linens and furniture. After the war, the responsibility to provide a house shifted to the bride. With land scarce, single women who owned a home received many offers of marriage.

Dress

Both Greek and Turkish Cypriots wear Western clothing. Today, traditional clothing is worn primarily at folk festivals or at demonstrations of traditional dances.

Education

After World War II, it became apparent that education offered young people many opportunities for advancement. As the value attached to education grew, families made a greater effort to provide it for their children, even if that meant moving to the city in order to be near secondary schools. Today, the literacy rate in both regions of the country has reached 97 percent.

Since 1974, Turkish Cypriots have developed a strong secular school system that provides education from primary school through the university level. Ironically, as the number of university graduates increases, so does the "brain drain," the loss of highly educated people who move elsewhere in search of better jobs, higher pay, or political stability. There just aren't enough jobs in the TRNC to support the number of graduates.

In 1990, Lefke University opened in the TRNC. Funded by the Islamic Development Bank, the university provides an advanced education while following Islamic principles. The university was originally planned for Turkey, but following a vigorous protest by secular groups, it was located in northern Cyprus instead. Some Turkish Cypriots welcome the arrival of an Islamic institution, while others fear that it will threaten the future of secular education in the TRNC.

Recreation and Leisure

With mountains, beaches, and an ocean to explore, it's no wonder that Cypriots spend much of their time out-of-doors. Winter and summer, the Troodos Mountains are a favorite destination. Hikes in the cool altitudes during the summer are refreshing after a hot week in the cities. With several beaches to choose from, Cypriots and their visitors enjoy swimming, snorkeling, and scuba diving. In the winter, the Troodos receive enough snow for downhill skiing. Soccer and basketball are the most popular sporting events in Cyprus.

The foods of Cyprus include dishes of both Greek and Turkish origin, such as moussaka *and* souvlakia.

Food

The food of Cyprus, not surprisingly, reflects the heritage of its Greek and Turkish cultures. Locally grown fruits and vegetables join fish and lamb on the tables of restaurants and homes alike.

Cypriot meals often begin with *meze* (muh-ZAY), or appetizers. At a restaurant, meze might include as many as twenty dishes, but fewer would be prepared for a family sitting down to eat at home. Diners generally eat only a bite or two from the various dishes if a full meal will be served, although some people order meze in place of a meal. Meze dishes include savory foods such as fresh vegetables, cheeses, *houmous* (ground chickpeas with olive oil and garlic, called *hummus* in other regions), fresh fish, shrimp, octopus, chicken, sausage, and bread. *Halloumi*, the traditional Cypriot cheese made from sheep's milk and mint, is usually grilled or fried and served as meze.

The main dishes on Cyprus are very similar to those in Greece and Turkey. Favorites include *moussaka* (moo-suh-KAH), a layered dish of lamb, potatoes, eggplant, and zucchini; *souvlakia* (soov-LAH-kee-uh) or *kebab* (kuh-BOB), roasted lamb wrapped in pita bread or served on rice; and *kleftiko*, lamb roasted in a traditional underground sealed oven. Stews that combine lamb, rabbit, or beef with vegetables are common, as are pilafs of cracked wheat and onions.

SOUVLAKIA

1 medium onion, cut into chunks (about 1-1/2 cups)
1-1/3 cups olive oil
1/3 cup fresh lemon juice
3 tablespoons minced garlic
3 tablespoons dried oregano
2 tablespoons freshly ground pepper
2-1/2 to 3 pounds leg of lamb, trimmed well and cut into 24 2-inch cubes
Salt

To make the marinade, puree the onions in a food processor. Add all other ingredients to the processor except the lamb and salt. Pulse just until combined.

Place the lamb cubes in a large plastic bag with a resealable top. Pour the marinade over the lamb and seal tightly. Refrigerate overnight, turning once or twice.

Heat the grill or broiler. Let the lamb warm to room temperature. Thread the cubes onto 6 skewers and lightly sprinkle with salt. Grill or broil 3 to 4 minutes on each side until medium-rare. Remove the lamb from the skewers and serve on top of a bed of rice pilaf, accompanied by a salad of diced cucumbers, yogurt, and mint.

Serves 6.

Source: *The Mediterranean Kitchen* by Joyce Goldstein.

Desserts range from ripe, juicy, freshly picked fruits to pastries sweetened with honey. *Baklava* (bah-kluh-VAH), a rich layered pastry full of honey and nuts, is a favorite of both Greek and Turkish Cypriots.

Holidays and Festivals

Religious Celebrations

Turkish Cypriot Muslims observe the same Islamic holy days and festivals as other Muslims. However, they use the Turkish names for the events. The most important festival is Kurban Bayrami, the Feast of the Sacrifice (Eid al-Adha). As in other Islamic countries, sheep are slaughtered in preparation for a feast that celebrates Allah's goodness in providing a rich bounty for his people. A certain portion of the meat is distributed to the poor during the three days of this festival.

Seker Bayrami, the Little Feast (Eid al-Fitr), marks the end of the holy month of Ramadan. The celebration begins as soon as the new moon is sighted at the end of Ramadan and continues for three days. Special foods and delicacies are prepared for the festivities and shared with friends and neighbors.

Easter, the celebration of Christ's resurrection, is the highlight of the Greek Orthodox year. Devout believers fast during Lent, the forty days before Easter, avoiding red meat, poultry, fish, and dairy products. During this period, individuals pray to strengthen their relationship with God. The week immediately preceding Easter is called Holy Week. Special church services mark this week, especially on Good Friday. Most businesses are closed on this day. Church members decorate a bier—a coffin on a stand—with gold cloth and flowers, then carry the bier in a funeral procession through the streets of the town or village. At midnight on Easter morning, people enter a darkened church. The priest emerges with a lighted candle and uses the flame to light a candle held by a person seated in the first row. The flame is passed from one member to another until light fills the church, symbolizing Christ's resurrection. People carefully carry their lighted candles home, where the flames bless their homes. A traditional soup called *mageiritsa* is served to break the fast. Each family member takes a turn rapping a red hard-boiled egg against another person's egg. Having the last uncracked egg brings luck in the coming year.

This Greek Cypriot attends to his candle during an Orthodox Easter mass. This 2003 service was held in a church in the Turkish-occupied area of Cyprus in the afternoon instead of at midnight when most Easter masses are celebrated because those in attendance had to be back in the Greek Cypriot–controlled area before nightfall.

Second only to Easter is the Christmas holiday. Compared to American and European traditions, the Greek Cypriot Christmas is relatively quiet. The season begins December 6, on Saint Nicholas's feast day, and lasts through Epiphany, January 6. Family members and friends exchange gifts on Saint Basil's Day, which is also New Year's Day.

A favorite Christmas activity is the *Kalanda*. On Christmas Eve, groups of children go from one house to the next asking if they can sing the *Kalanda* (Christmas carols). The singing of the *Kalanda* is considered a blessing to each household, so those who are thus honored usually offer gifts to the singers.

Another Christmas tradition arises from the belief that *kalikatzaroi*, little demons or goblins, visit earth between Christmas and Epiphany to play tricks, such as extinguishing fires. Because they enter through the chimney, Greek Cypriots keep a fire burning day and night during this period. Basil and holy water also offer protection from the demons, so many people use a cross to sprinkle the rooms of their homes with the protective mixture.

The Arts

The arts on Cyprus are dominated by folk art and handcrafts, the rich traditions of an ancient people.

Traditional Arts

Since antiquity, Cyprus has been recognized for the quality and creativity of its craftspeople. Early Cypriot metalworkers were known for their skill in crafting armor and swords—Alexander the Great carried a

SAINT NICHOLAS, THE SAILOR'S PROTECTOR

Saint Nicholas, the patron saint of sailors, travelers, bakers, merchants, and children, is often thought of as an early version of Santa Claus by children in Europe and America. But Greek Cypriots consider his role as the patron saint of sailors as his most important responsibility. They believe that his beard always drips with the spray from the ocean as he battles to save ships at sea from sinking.

Although protection at sea comes first, Saint Nicholas also plays a part in Greek Cypriot Christmas traditions. The tradition of giving gifts at Christmas began with Saint Nicholas, known for his kindness to children and his gifts to the poor. (The Dutch name for Saint Nicholas is *Sinterklaas*, which became Santa Claus in English.) The Christmas season in Cyprus begins on December 6, Saint Nicholas's feast day.

sword that was made in Cyprus. The skill of Cypriot women in textile arts such as making lace and weaving is still celebrated today and potters continue a tradition that began thousands of years ago. Sadly, many of Cyprus's traditional crafts are slowly dying out. Many master craftspeople are in their seventies and eighties, and few young people are willing to learn the ancient crafts because they do not bring in enough income to justify the long hours.

Metal Crafts

The word *copper* comes from the Greeks' name for Cyprus, a revered source of the precious metal. During ancient times, much of Cyprus's copper was exported to foreign countries, but coppersmiths also hammered sheets of copper into cooking pots, ladles, and other household objects. (Anything that comes into contact with food must be lined with tin; the copper is poisonous.) At one time, coppersmiths traveled from village to village repairing copperware and selling new pans, but today most coppersmiths create decorative copper pieces for tourists.

While Cyprus is best known for its copper work, silversmiths in the village of Lefkara create delicate filigree work, as well as reproductions of antique silver serving pieces.

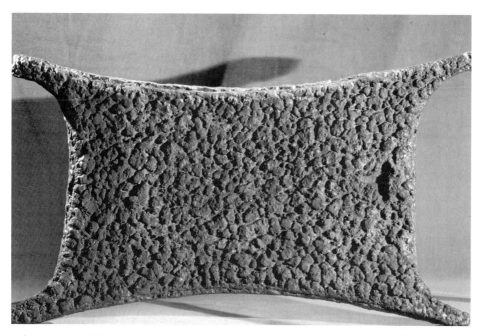

An example of Cyprus's long association with copper crafts, this copper ingot from around the fourteenth century B.C.E. is on display at a museum of antiquities in Cyprus. Ingots like these would have been melted down and used by artisans to make tools or other objects.

Textile Arts

Following the fall of the Byzantine Empire, Cyprus was the only Christian stronghold in the eastern Mediterranean. Consequently, the art of creating intricately woven and embroidered textiles for Christian religious services moved to Cyprus. The modern techniques used in making Lefkara lace, or Lefkaritika, were introduced by the Venetians in the late fifteenth century.

Today, the women of Lefkara, a village in south-central Cyprus, are known for their exquisite lace-embroidery work. Women often gather outside their homes to work on this traditional craft. Using Irish linen, the women count the threads and draw them together or cover them with embroidery floss, creating intricate open designs in white, ecru, or brown.

Large flocks of sheep on Cyprus provide the wool needed to sustain the tradition of hand-woven textiles. Women from many villages weave rugs, tapestries, curtains, and other items using centuries-old patterns and textures.

These women are participating in an art that has been familiar in Cyprus for centuries: the making of lace. The women of the village of Lefkara, in particular, are known for their exquisite lace-making skills.

Pottery

Ancient pottery techniques are still practiced today by women in Kornos, a village near Nicosia, while in other regions craftspeople create modern pottery decorated with ancient designs.

Visual Arts

In addition to the pottery created in a traditional manner, contemporary Cypriot artists, such as Gregoris Lagos and Kyriacos Lyras, use mosaics and watercolors to create colorful impressions of everyday scenes.

Theater and Film

Cyprus's major cities, especially those in the Republic of Cyprus, support many theaters. Productions range from ancient Greek drama and Shakespeare to plays by modern Western playwrights. Cinemas offer the latest in European and American films.

Music and Dance

Contemporary Cypriot folk music builds upon the musical traditions of Greek and Byzantine music. Well-known traditional tunes form the basis of many folk songs; the lyrics are changed to create each new *laika*, or song. Some of the basic tunes are reserved for special occasions such as weddings, some are used only in religious services, and others accompany traditional dances. The folk dances of Greece have been adapted on Cyprus as well. Men traditionally danced in a variety of settings, while women were restricted to dancing at weddings. The only occasion when men and women were allowed to dance together was at their own wedding ceremony. Today's Cypriot folk societies keep the traditional dances alive.

Greek Cypriot orchestras traditionally include a variety of stringed instruments, such as the violin, the *bouzouki*, the *laouto*, and the guitar. The bouzouki is a stringed instrument, similar to a lute. It originally had three double strings, but a fourth string was added around 1900 to add a greater musical range. The *laouto*, a lute with a bigger body and smaller neck than the bouzouki, has four strings and is played with a feather.

Literature

Cypriot writers have long been valued by their fellow citizens, but there has been a literary renaissance of sorts in recent years. Since 1969, the government has awarded prizes for outstanding poetry, novels, short stories, and essays. Special awards honor new writers; winners of the Young Cypriot Writer award get to have their books published.

THE MYTH OF APHRODITE AND ADONIS

Aphrodite (known as Venus to the Romans) was the Greek goddess of love and beauty. She rose from the Mediterranean Sea fully formed and stepped out of her seashell on the coast of Cyprus. People everywhere marveled at her beauty. Her worshipers built a temple to honor Aphrodite near the village of Paphos in southwestern Cyprus. Pilgrims visited this temple for centuries.

Living on Cyprus was a handsome youth named Adonis. He was a great hunter, afraid of nothing. As Adonis prepared to go hunting one day, Aphrodite tried to persuade him to avoid wild boars and other dangerous animals. While roaming the countryside, Adonis came across a wild boar. Ignoring Aphrodite's request, he threw his spear, wounding the boar but not killing it. Suddenly, the boar turned and attacked Adonis. Gored in the side, Adonis bled to death.

Aphrodite was heartbroken to learn of Adonis's death. In the spring, however, near the spot where Adonis fell grew a new flower. These flowers, called anemones or wind flowers, were as red as blood. The flowers still grow on Cyprus today, reminding its people of the great love of Aphrodite for Adonis.

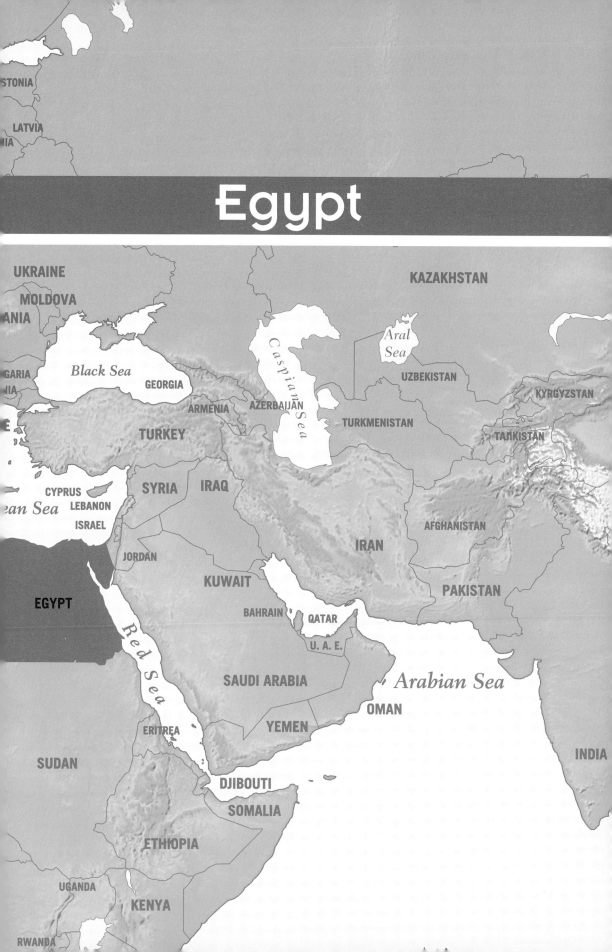

Egypt

Mention Egypt and visions of ancient empires, pharaohs, and pyramids come to mind. While Egypt's 6,000-year-old civilization attracts much interest, the country provides vital leadership in the Middle East today.

Egypt's strategic location in the northeast corner of Africa, with the only land link between Africa and Asia, made it an economic power in early times. Its importance as a shortcut between Europe and Asia only increased when the Suez Canal was built in the mid-nineteenth century. Throughout history, outside powers that wanted to expand or protect their own economic interests sought to control Egypt's rivers, canals, and land routes to Asia.

The Egyptians

Egypt's location at the junction of Africa and Asia, along with its wealth and resources, made it a center of commerce throughout history. Traders from Europe and Asia made their way to ancient Egypt, along with invading forces from Greece, Rome, Turkey, and Arabia. As a result, people of many races and ethnic groups made Egypt their home. Today, through intermarriage and the widespread adoption of the Arabic language and culture, the descendants of these diverse groups have created a unique Egyptian identity.

FAST FACTS

✔ **Official name:** Arab Republic of Egypt

✔ **Capital:** Cairo

✔ **Location:** Northeastern Africa, between Libya and the Gaza Strip

✔ **Area:** 386,662 square miles (1,001,454 square kilometers)

✔ **Population:** 70,712,345 (July 2002 estimate)

✔ **Age distribution:**
0–14 years: 34%
15–64 years: 62%
over 65 years: 4%

✔ **Life expectancy:**
Males: 62 years
Females: 66 years

✔ **Ethnic groups:** Egyptian, Bedouin Arab, and Berber 99%, Greek, Nubian, Armenian, and other European 1%

✔ **Religions:** Muslim 94%, Coptic Christian and other 6%

✔ **Languages:** Arabic is the official language; English and French are taught in school

✔ **Currency:** Egyptian pound (EGP)
US$1.00 = 5.74 EGP (2003)

✔ **Average annual income:** US$1,490

✔ **Major exports:** Crude oil, petroleum products, cotton

Source: CIA, *The World Factbook 2002;* BBC News Country Profiles.

Even though a strong national identity has been forged through the centuries, several cultural groups, including the Nubians, Bedouins, and Copts, have maintained their traditions and languages.

The Nubians

The Nubians are one of the oldest cultural groups in the Nile River Valley. Their ancient kingdoms were located in what is now southern Egypt and northern Sudan. As traders and artisans, the Nubians enjoyed many periods of prosperity. In fact, their name comes from the ancient Egyptian word for gold, since the Nubian traders were the main source of gold for the Egyptian pharaohs. Copper and stone from Nubia were also valued by the ancient Egyptians.

Historically, Nubian villages were established along the Nile from the city of Aswan southward into Sudan. In 1902, the British built a dam just south of Aswan to control flooding and to aid in irrigation of crops. Many Nubian men moved to urban areas in order to find work to support their families. Six decades later, the Aswan High Dam was built, increasing the amount of land that could be cultivated and doubling the supply of electricity. The 311 miles (500 kilometers) of Lake Nasser, which formed behind the High Dam, submerged much of the Nubian homeland, including ancient temples and pyramids and present-day homes and mosques. Once again, there was an influx of Nubian men seeking work in Egypt's urban areas. Their families usually stayed behind in government-sponsored housing.

Today, although many Nubian men live and work in cities such as Cairo and Alexandria, the group works to maintain its traditional village culture. Despite being uprooted and relocated, the Nubians have guarded their own cultural traditions and language. Few Nubians marry outside of their cultural or ethnic group, and the Nubian language is spoken in addition to Arabic. In the 1970s, some families began moving back to Nubia. Since then, four villages with traditional mud houses have been established along the shores of Lake Nasser.

The Bedouins

The Bedouins, nomadic Arabs living in the Western and Eastern Deserts and the Sinai Peninsula, share a common language—Arabic—with most Egyptians. They have a unique culture and history, however, which sets them apart from other groups.

Starting in the nineteenth century, the Egyptian government used incentives of farmland to persuade Bedouins to give up their traditional nomadic life in order to settle and farm in one place. A nomadic life involves people and animals moving from place to place to follow water and food supplies.

Traditionally, each clan, or extended family unit, of Bedouins claimed a particular territory. The group moved from place to place within this territory, following the grazing and water that were available during each season. Homes were generally tents made of cloth woven from goat or camel hair.

In the nineteenth and twentieth centuries, the Egyptian government offered incentives for the Bedouins to leave their nomadic lifestyle and settle in a permanent location. Gradually, most Bedouins accepted the offers of farmland and adopted a sedentary way of life. Although still some Bedouins continue to move their goats from one pasture to another each season, they have abandoned some elements of tradition. Today, pickup trucks are as likely to be used to move the animals to pasture as camels were in the past.

The Copts

Copts are members of Egypt's largest Christian community. When Muslims conquered Egypt in the seventh century, the local population spoke Coptic and belonged to the Coptic Church. Over the centuries, however, most of the Egyptian population converted to Islam, and Arabic came to replace Coptic as the dominant language. Today, Copts make up about 6 percent of Egypt's population and live mostly in the villages and towns of Upper Egypt. The Coptic language is used only in religious settings.

Other Groups

Many Greeks moved to Egypt, especially around Alexandria, during the fourth century B.C.E. Their descendants still live primarily in Alexandria, although some Greeks live in Cairo as well. As the largest non-Arab minority group in Egypt, the Greeks retain their cultural and religious traditions. The Greek influence on Egyptian culture is still seen in the Coptic language, which records the ancient Egyptian language using Greek characters, as well as in the arts. Many Greeks are Coptic Christians.

Other ethnic groups include the Armenians, who live primarily in Cairo, and the Berbers. The Berbers are a nomadic people who live in the Western Desert region. Although they are Muslims, they speak a language unrelated to Arabic.

Land and Resources

About 95 percent of Egypt is desert and largely uninhabited. The stark desert landscape is divided by the mighty Nile River, which runs north through Egypt and empties into the Mediterranean Sea. Both the Nile and the surrounding deserts helped shape Egypt into one of the ancient world's greatest civilizations, and both still play a major role in Egyptian life today. A rapidly growing population has created immense pressure on Egypt's natural resources, including the Nile. Air and water pollution are serious problems in many parts of the country.

Geography

Egypt, which includes the Sinai Peninsula, is a nearly rectangular nation in the northeastern corner of Africa, stretching 636 miles (1,024 kilometers) from north to south and 771 miles (1,240 kilometers) from east to west. It covers 386,662 square miles (1,001,454 square kilometers), an area about the size of New Mexico and Texas combined.

THE NILE RIVER

The Nile River is the longest river in the world, running northward 4,180 miles (6,688 kilometers) from its sources in Uganda and Ethiopia through Egypt. As it approaches the Mediterranean Sea, the Nile spreads across a delta that covers an area about the size of Massachusetts. The river has always been a lifeline for Egypt, providing most of the fresh water found in the country.

Historically, whenever the Nile flooded, layers of mud were deposited over the land on either side of the river. This process made the Nile River Valley so fertile that enough food could be grown to support the entire country, even though the region covers only 3.5 percent of Egypt. Today, the Aswan High Dam and other dams along the Nile control the flooding and the damage that often accompanied it. They also limit the amount of silt that is carried by the Nile, reducing the agricultural productivity of the floodplains and contributing to the erosion of the riverbanks in Upper (southern) Egypt.

The beauty and human history of the Nile have always captured people's imaginations. This view shows a famous hotel on the river in Aswan.

However, nearly all of Egypt's people live along the Nile Valley and Delta region—an area smaller than West Virginia.

Egypt has more than 1,802 miles (2,900 kilometers) of coastline. The Mediterranean Sea forms Egypt's northern border, while the Gulf of Suez, the Gulf of Aqaba, and the Red Sea border the Sinai Peninsula and the mainland's eastern border. The Sinai Peninsula, a triangular piece of land, extends from Egypt's northeastern corner. The Gaza Strip and Israel share the eastern border of the Sinai Peninsula, while Libya and Sudan border Egypt on the west and south, respectively.

There are four major regions within Egypt: the Nile Valley and Delta, the Western (Libyan) Desert, the Eastern (Arabian) Desert, and the Sinai Peninsula. The lush green of the Nile Valley and Delta region, which represents less than 4 percent of the country, contrasts vividly with the surrounding deserts. The water from the river, along with the rich silt that it deposits in the flood plains each year, makes agriculture and permanent settlements possible. Not surprisingly, the Nile Valley and Delta is the most populated region, with about 99 percent of Egyptians living there.

To the west of the Nile Valley is the Western, or Libyan, Desert. Its sandy, flat lands include several low-lying areas called *depressions*. Six of the depressions are oases, locations with fresh water that comes from underground sources or, in the case of the Fayyoum depression, the

A DIFFERENT KIND OF ISLAND

Mention desert islands and most people will picture an isolated piece of land surrounded by water. But there are also "islands" in the deserts of Egypt—islands of green grasses, fruit and vegetable farms, trees, and even lakes, made possible by underground water sources that rise up to the surface. These islands are called *oases* (oh-AY-seez). Although many Westerners picture an oasis as a small body of water surrounded by palm trees, many oases are quite large, with one or more villages within their borders.

The Eastern, or Arabian, Desert stretches eastward from the Nile. In contrast to the Western Desert, the Eastern Desert is rocky and mountainous. Few people live in this region. The Eastern Desert's biggest contribution to the Egyptian economy is its oil deposits.

The Sinai Peninsula is situated at the northeastern corner of Egypt, where it links Africa and Asia. The southern two-thirds of the peninsula is covered with mountains, including Mount Catherine, which is the highest point in Egypt at 8,625 feet (2,630 meters). Oases and freshwater wells made trade routes across the peninsula possible in ancient times, and many support limited settlements today.

Nile. The seventh and largest depression—the Qattara—offers only saltwater. With a low spot that lies 436 feet (130 meters) below sea level, the Qattara depression is the lowest point in Egypt.

Major Cities

All of Egypt's major cities are located in the Nile Valley and Delta region. Cairo, the capital and largest city in Egypt, was built more than ten centuries ago at the point where the Nile branches out into the delta. Egyptian cities have been located at this spot for over 3,500 years. Cairo has experienced such prolonged periods of rapid growth that housing construction has not been able to keep up. Today about 20 percent of Egypt's population lives in Cairo and its sprawling suburbs. In addition to being the most important city in Egypt, Cairo is an influential city in the Islamic world.

The city of Alexandria, situated on the Mediterranean coast, was established by Alexander the Great when he conquered Egypt over 2,300 years ago. Today, Alexandria is the second-largest city in Egypt and serves as its key port. Oil refineries and textile mills are among the industries that keep Alexandria vital. In recent years, Alexandria has become popular as a resort during the hot summer months.

Climate

Egypt is mostly desert, with a hot dry climate. The northern coastal region receives the most rainfall, and even that is minimal, averaging slightly less than 8 inches (20 centimeters) each year. Some areas in southern Egypt may go years without receiving any rain.

Summers are extremely hot inland, with temperatures reaching 109° F (43° C) during the day. Temperatures drop dramatically at night, as

A TWENTIETH-CENTURY PROBLEM

By the mid-1990s, Cairo had some of the worst air pollution in the world. The high lead levels were particularly dangerous, suspected of causing up to 20,000 deaths each year. Over the past decade, the U.S. Agency for International Development (USAID) has funded programs designed by the Egyptian government to test air quality and reduce pollution. Some measures have been fairly simple: frequent automotive tune-ups and the use of unleaded gasoline. Other programs have introduced stringent guidelines for Cairo's many industries.

low as 45° F (7° C). The northern coastal areas are slightly cooler due to breezes from the Mediterranean Sea, so daytime temperatures generally stay below 86° F (30° C).

Temperatures don't vary quite as widely during the winter months of November through April. The desert areas may reach freezing temperatures at night, then warm up to 64° F (18° C). Once again, the northern coast experiences milder temperatures, generally getting no colder than 57° F (14° C).

In the spring, hot dry winds called *khamsin* blast Egypt. The khamsin sweep sand and dust from the east and blow it westward at speeds up to 87 miles (140 kilometers) per hour. Temperatures may rise nearly 70° F (39° C) in a few hours when the khamsin are blowing. Whenever possible, Egyptians remain inside when the khamsin arrive.

Natural Resources

Egypt's most vital resource is the Nile River, the major source of fresh water for the country. Over the past several decades, the quality of water has deteriorated. The Aswan High Dam, built to store and use the river's water for cultivation, has indirectly contributed to the declining water quality. The floods that once regularly occurred along the Nile deposited thick layers of rich silt, full of nutrients, on the floodplain. This fertile soil nourished the farmers' crops. Today, with the silt captured behind the dam, farmers must use chemical fertilizers to produce adequate crop yields. Many farmers also use herbicides (weed killers) and pesticides (insect killers). All of these compounds run off into the Nile, creating

THE SHIP OF THE DESERT

Camels are amazing animals, perfectly suited for life in the desert. Their thick, rubbery mouths enable camels to eat tough, thorny plants that are inedible to most animals. The camel's hump stores fatty deposits that can be drawn upon for energy when food is not readily available. Excess water is stored in the bloodstream, allowing camels to go several days without water. The hot sand can't scorch the thick, padded soles of the camel's feet. And when the sand blows, the camel's thick eyelashes and nostrils that can close completely keep the sand out.

Most camels in Egypt are dromedary, or Arabian, camels with one hump. The Bedouins and Berbers who still follow a traditional nomadic way of life generally saddle and ride the camels, often traveling 100 miles (160 kilometers) a day. However, the camels that were once such a vital part of life in the desert are slowly being replaced by pickup trucks.

water pollution. Other sources of pollution include poorly regulated industries that have grown up along the Nile, untreated sewage, and wastewater from the cities that are located near the Nile.

Other important natural resources are the mineral deposits found throughout Egypt. In ancient times, the gold mined in Lower Egypt was highly valued. Today, the oil reserves in the Eastern Desert and the Sinai Peninsula have replaced gold as the most valuable resource. Other important minerals that are exploited are phosphates, iron ore, uranium, and natural gas.

Plants and Animals

As might be expected, most of Egypt's plant and animal life is found in the Nile Valley and Delta region. Date palms grow all along the Nile, as well as in the desert oases. Tamarisk, eucalyptus, acacia, jacaranda, and carob trees also grow in these same areas. Flowers and grasses thrive wherever water is available. Papyrus reed, used by ancient Egyptians to make paper, is increasingly rare.

Wildlife also abounds near the Nile. Perhaps the most diverse group is the birds, with over 300 species—including the ibis and flamingo—making their home in Egypt at least part of the year. The Nile crocodiles, once widespread, nearly disappeared from the region. In recent years, however, they have been spotted in Lake Nasser.

The desert regions have fewer species of animals, but those who live there are well suited to the heat and limited water. The camel is particularly well adapted to the desert environment, with the ability to withstand several days without food or water. The sand cat, which is thought to be the ancestor of the domesticated housecat, has thick furry pads on its feet that provide protection from the burning sand. It obtains enough moisture to survive by eating small rodents and snakes.

Reptiles and insects are also found in the desert regions. Some snakes, such as the cobras and vipers, are poisonous. One, the spitting cobra, doesn't even have to bite its prey; it can spit its venom up to 12 feet (3.6 meters) away. Scorpions, which can inflict a painful sting, are found throughout Egypt.

History

Ancient Days

People first began settling in the Nile Valley about 6,000 years ago. Originally hunter-gatherers, the people soon took advantage of the rich soil in the floodplains of the Nile to cultivate crops of wheat and barley. Various tribes established villages that were ruled by leaders called *headmen*. This new hierarchical power structure set the stage for the highly organized kingdoms that emerged in Upper (southern) and Lower (northern) Egypt.

According to tradition, the two kingdoms were united by the first Egyptian pharaoh (FAIR-oh)—King Menes—around 3100 B.C.E. Egyptian mythology after this time combines the stories of both regions and establishes the belief that the pharaohs, or kings, were reincarnations of the Egyptian god Horus, son of Osiris and Isis. (Ancient Egyptians believed that a person's soul doesn't die. Rather, it is reincarnated or reborn in a new human body after the person's death.)

Foreign Domination Begins

The last Egyptian pharaoh was conquered in 525 B.C.E. by invading Persian forces. Persian rulers in Egypt called themselves pharaohs, but Egypt was ruled as a province of the Persian Empire from 525 B.C.E.

LIFE IN ANCIENT EGYPT

Ancient Egyptians developed a civilization so rich and creative that its influences are still seen in modern life. Their innovations in engineering, agriculture, writing, sailing, and the arts impressed visitors and conquerors of their time—and still amaze people today.

The early Egyptians' dependence upon the Nile fostered many of their achievements. For example, they developed an irrigation system that enabled them to grow more crops. They studied the stars and planets in order to create a calendar that would let them know when the river would flood each year. Our calendar is still based upon their division of time into years containing twelve months and 365 days.

The pyramids and temple complexes built by the early pharaohs are remarkable for their architectural and engineering techniques. The Age of the Pyramids (2700–2200 B.C.E.) saw over seventy pyramids constructed. They were built out of huge blocks of rock, the largest of which weighed 15 tons (13.5 metric tons)—more than two elephants. The rocks were perfectly cut and moved into place by human labor, without the help of wheels. These giant monuments served as tombs for the pharaohs, with room for all the items they would need after death.

IMPORTANT EVENTS IN EGYPT'S HISTORY

6000 B.C.E.	People begin settling along the Nile.
3100 B.C.E.	King Menes unites Upper and Lower Egypt and establishes the rule by pharaohs.
2700 B.C.E.	Age of the Pyramids begins.
525 B.C.E.	Egypt becomes part of the Persian Empire.
404 B.C.E.	Egyptians regain independence.
343 B.C.E.	Persians conquer Egypt once more.
332 B.C.E.	Alexander the Great defeats the Persians and adds Egypt to his growing empire.
323 B.C.E.	Ptolemaic dynasty begins.
30 B.C.E.	Cleopatra, last of the Ptolemy rulers, commits suicide when Egypt becomes part of the Roman Empire.
60 C.E.	Christianity is established in Egypt.
451	Coptic Church splits from the Catholic Church.
641	Arabs conquer Egypt and introduce Islamic and Arab culture.
969	Fatimid dynasty is established in Egypt; Cairo becomes the capital.
1171	Saladin overthrows the Fatimids and establishes the Ayyubid dynasty in Egypt and Syria.
1250	Mamluks rise to power.
1260	Mamluk ruler Qutuz and his army stop the advance of Mongol forces.
1517	Ottoman Empire conquers Egypt.
mid-1700s	Mamluks return to power although Egypt remains part of the Ottoman Empire.
1798	Napoleon invades Egypt, capturing Alexandria and Cairo.
1801	The British and Ottomans join forces to drive the French out of Egypt.
1805	Muhammad Ali becomes the viceroy (governor) of Egypt.
1859	Construction of the Suez Canal begins.
1863	Ismail Pasha rules Egypt from 1863 to 1879 and implements many reforms.
1869	Suez Canal opens.

1879	Ismail is forced from power. His son Tawfiq replaces him as khedive.
1881	Nationalist political parties form.
1882	Britain occupies Egypt and secures control of the Suez Canal.
1914	Britain declares Egypt a British protectorate.
1919	Egyptians protest against the British decision to exile nationalist leaders.
1922	Britain grants Egypt limited independence.
1936	King Farouk I ascends to power following the death of his father.
1948	Jewish state of Israel is established.
1952	King Farouk is overthrown.
1954	Gamal Abdel Nasser assumes leadership of Egyptian government.
1956	Suez Canal is nationalized to help pay for construction of the Aswan High Dam; Britain, France, and Israel invade Egypt.
1967	Egyptian army is defeated in the Six-Day War with Israel.
1970	Aswan High Dam is completed; Israel, Jordan, and Egypt sign a cease-fire agreement; Nasser dies; Anwar Sadat becomes president.
1973	Arab-Israeli War (Yom Kippur War).
1974	Peace talks begin between Egypt and Israel.
1978	Sadat receives the Nobel Peace Prize for his role in ending hostilities between Egypt and Israel.
1979	Egypt and Israel sign a peace agreement; Arab countries institute an economic boycott in protest.
1981	Sadat is assassinated; Hosni Mubarak becomes president.
1987	Egypt restores relations with other Arab countries.
1990	Egypt supports the alliance to expel Iraq from Kuwait during the Persian Gulf War.
1995	Mubarak escapes an assassination attempt. Terrorists attack tourists, Copts, and politicians.

until the Egyptians threw off Persian rule in 404 B.C.E. The Persians regained control of Egypt in 343 B.C.E.

The Egyptians were freed from Persian rule when Alexander the Great, the young conqueror from Macedonia (in present-day Greece), defeated the Persians in 332 B.C.E. He was welcomed by the Egyptians, who saw similarities between the Greek gods and their own. Alexander founded the city of Alexandria, which soon became known throughout the Mediterranean region as a center of learning.

Following Alexander's death nearly ten years later, one of his generals—Ptolemy (TAH-luh-mee)—assumed leadership in Egypt. Ptolemy and his descendants ruled Egypt for nearly three centuries. The last—and most famous—Ptolemaic (tah-luh-MAY-ik) ruler was Cleopatra, who committed suicide when the Romans defeated Egypt and added it to the Roman Empire in 30 B.C.E.

The Roman Empire ruled over Egypt as a province for nearly 600 years. During this time, much of Egypt's wealth and crops was sent to the emperor of Rome. Christianity arrived in Egypt early in the first century and spread southward. Egyptian Christians were called Copts or

Christianity became the official religion of the Roman Empire, which included Egypt, in the fourth century. This silver coin was made to mark the occasion. It features a portrait of Roman emperor Constantine the Great on one side and a depiction of the goddess Roma on the other.

Coptic Christians, after the Greek word for *Egyptian*. The Roman emperor Diocletian believed that Christianity threatened the strength and unity of the Roman Empire. In 303, he ordered the enslavement of most Christians and the destruction of Christian churches and schools throughout Egypt. This harsh persecution lasted for three years.

After Constantine the Great became emperor of Rome, he made Christianity the official state religion but declared that there would be tolerance for all religions. During this period, many Egyptians converted to Christianity and the Coptic Church became very powerful. After the fall of Rome late in the fourth century, Egypt came under control of the Byzantine (BIZ-uhn-teen) Empire (formerly the Eastern Roman Empire). In 451, the Coptic Church came into conflict with the Byzantine church leaders over the nature of Christ; that is, how to describe Christ's human and divine aspects. Unable to agree, the churches split. The Byzantine Church attempted to force the Coptic

This handwritten manuscript of the Qur'an from the seventh century is one of the oldest vestiges of the presence of Islam in Egypt. It was the first book to be placed on the shelves of a new library that opened in Alexandria in 2002.

Church to adopt Byzantine beliefs. When that didn't work, the Coptic Christians were brutally persecuted, many of them tortured or killed. By the time Islamic armies swept into Egypt two hundred years later, most Egyptians welcomed any change that would rid their country of the hated Byzantine rulers.

The Arrival of Islam

In 639, Arab armies arrived in Egypt with the goal of conquering the Byzantine land and adding Egypt to the Islamic world. The Byzantine armies resisted the advance of the Arabs, but by 641, Egypt was part of a vast *caliphate,* or Islamic kingdom. Egyptians were given the choice of converting to Islam or paying taxes for the privilege of following another religion. Over time many Egyptians converted to Islam, but some Copts chose to remain Christians. Steadily, Islam became the predominant religion, and the Arabic language was adopted in all areas of society, including business and government.

For over three centuries, Egypt was ruled by Islamic governors who followed Sunni tradition. All this changed in 969, when the Fatimid dynasty was established in Egypt. The Fatimids claimed that they were descendants of Fatima, the Prophet Mohammad's daughter and wife of Ali, the founder of Shi'a Islam. Under Fatimid rule, the city of Cairo was established as the capital of the Shi'a caliphate. It soon became known as a center of learning as well, where Shi'ite religious leaders and teachers gathered to clarify and define Shi'a doctrine (beliefs).

In 1171, Salah al-Din ibn Ayyub—a Kurdish general known in the West as Saladin (SAH-luh-deen)—overthrew the Fatimids and established the Ayyubid dynasty in Egypt and Syria. A Sunni Muslim himself, Saladin returned Egypt to the Abbasid caliphate, the Sunni-based caliphate that was ruled from Baghdad (in present-day Iraq). Cairo continued to gain status as a center of Islamic studies. In 1187, Saladin led forces that drove the Christian Crusaders from Jerusalem and Palestine. The Crusaders responded by directing attacks on Egypt during the first half of the thirteenth century. These attacks weakened the Ayyubid dynasty, so much so that a group of Turkish slave-soldiers known as Mamluks were able to take control of Egypt and Syria when the last Ayyubid ruler died in 1250.

The Mamluks ruled from 1250 to 1517. Invading Mongol armies from eastern Asia destroyed the Abbasid caliphate in Baghdad in 1258. The Mamluks, however, were able to stop the advance of the Mongols and retain control of Egypt and Syria. They maintained one of the most prominent states of the medieval Middle East.

In 1517, the armies of the Ottoman Empire defeated the Mamluks and added Egypt to their empire. Although the Ottomans placed governors in Egypt to rule over the province, the Mamluks never gave up their struggle to regain power. In the course of the eighteenth century, the Mamluk leaders gradually took control of Egypt. They even refused to send the taxes from the province to the Ottoman leader in Istanbul.

A Growing European Influence

Napoleon Bonaparte, a French general, invaded Egypt in 1798. He hoped to establish a base in the Middle East from which he could disrupt British influence in the region. France also wanted to exploit Egypt's commercial possibilities. Napoleon was able to capture Alexandria and Cairo, but much of Egypt remained under the control of

Muhammad Ali was an officer in the Ottoman army who rose to power and became viceroy of Egypt in 1805. He attempted to gain Egypt's independence from the Ottoman Empire, but was pushed back by European forces who feared that a strong, independent Egypt would threaten trade.

the Mamluks. Thousands of Egyptians, led by Islamic religious leaders, protested the French presence in Cairo. The British and Ottomans joined forces to drive the French out of Egypt, an effort that was successful in 1801.

The Ottoman army remained in Egypt following the departure of the French troops. One officer, Muhammad Ali, rapidly ascended to power, becoming the viceroy (governor) of Egypt in 1805. Within six years, Muhammad Ali was in control of Egypt and had the full support of both the religious leaders and the urban elite.

Under Muhammad Ali's direction, Egypt expanded its agricultural exports. The income from cash crops such as cotton and sugarcane was used to establish textile factories and other industries, as well as to strengthen the military. With a strong economy and military in place, Muhammad Ali planned to break away from the Ottoman Empire.

The British and French governments were alarmed at these developments, particularly the Egyptian trade policies that prohibited the import of some foreign products. These trade embargoes threatened British and French commercial interests in the region. Both European powers preferred an intact, but weak, Ottoman Empire that welcomed their presence rather than a strong, independent Egypt that could wreck the economic advantages they held in the Middle East.

In 1831, Muhammad Ali invaded Syria (then a part of the Ottoman Empire). As he moved toward the Ottoman capital of Istanbul (formerly Constantinople) in 1840, five European powers—Britain, France, Austria, Russia, and Prussia—joined together to help the Ottoman government fend off the Egyptian army. As part of the treaty allowing Muhammad Ali to retain control of Egypt, he had to agree to open Egyptian markets to British goods. This agreement ultimately ruined the Egyptian textile industry. Muhammad Ali ruled Egypt—which remained a province in the Ottoman Empire—until 1848, a year before his death.

Descendants of Muhammad Ali ruled Egypt until 1952. The land ownership laws put into place during the reign of Muhammad Ali transferred much of the land that the peasants had used for subsistence farming to members of the noble family and the upper class. Thousands of peasants migrated to urban areas in search of work during the mid- to late nineteenth century. One of the projects that many of these peasants worked on was the Suez Canal.

Ismail Pasha (is-MAH-eel PAH-shuh), the grandson of Muhammad Ali, ruled Egypt from 1863 to 1879. He was given the royal title *khedive* (kuh-DEEV) by the Ottoman government as a reward for his contributions to the empire. Ismail shared many of his grandfather's economic and strategic goals, and to that end, he borrowed money from European banks, often at high interest rates, to modernize Egypt. Unfortunately, the cost of the railroads, bridges, telegraph lines, and other improvements that Khedive Ismail implemented, as well as wasteful expenditures, far exceeded Egypt's income from cotton exports. By 1875, Egypt was deeply in debt to foreign countries with no way to repay the money.

THE SUEZ CANAL

The Suez Canal is not the first manmade waterway linking the Mediterranean and the Red Sea. In fact, during ancient times, canals linked the Nile River with the Red Sea, offering a route from the Mediterranean region to India. This early navigational shortcut had been abandoned for centuries by the time construction on the Suez Canal started in 1859.

Said Pasha (sah-EED PAH-shah), the ruler of Egypt at the time, agreed to let French engineer Ferdinand de Lesseps build the canal, which is 104 miles (167 kilometers) long. The agreement was not very profitable for Egypt, however. Egyptian laborers were forced to work on the canal for little or no pay, while de Lesseps was granted the right to run the canal for ninety-nine years. During that time, Egypt received little of the money that the canal generated.

The Suez Canal has been at the center of several political disputes and wars. In 1956, the Suez Crisis erupted when president Gamal Nasser announced that Egypt would nationalize, or take control of, the Suez Canal. Britain, France, and Israel promptly invaded Egypt in hopes of protecting their own interests in the canal, but within a week all three countries were forced to withdraw their troops following demands by the United Nations. The Suez Canal was captured and closed by Israeli forces in 1967 during the Six-Day War. Six years later, Egypt took back the canal following the Arab-Israeli War. The Suez Canal reopened in 1975 and has remained open ever since.

By 2000, about fifty ships were crossing the Suez Canal each day. However, since terrorist attacks in the United States in 2001, boat traffic—and thus revenues—have slowed significantly.

Construction on the Suez Canal began in 1859, and it was opened for navigation in 1869. Most of the labor was provided by Egyptians, who were paid little or nothing.

Egypt was forced to allow European oversight of its debt payments. Before long, Europeans held many government positions. The Egyptian army officers and members of the upper class protested this development, and Ismail supported their demands to make the foreigners accountable to the Egyptian Assembly of Delegates—a group of respected Egyptians who had little actual political power. The Europeans countered by asking the Ottoman Empire to replace Ismail with a new ruler, which it did in 1879, appointing Ismail's son Tawfiq as khedive. Under Tawfiq's rule, European influence expanded.

Many members of the upper class, as well as officers in the Egyptian army, were dismayed by the treatment of Ismail and the growing presence of Europeans in their government. Secret societies that promoted Egyptian nationalism began forming. In 1881, two of the major *nationalist* groups joined together to form the National Popular Party. By 1882, the nationalists controlled the Assembly of Delegates and the army. Britain and France demanded that Tawfiq exile the leaders of the nationalists. Riots broke out as Egyptians protested European intervention in Egyptian affairs. The British responded by invading the country; by September 1882, British forces were occupying Egypt. The occupation would continue for more than half a century.

> *Nationalists* believe that their country should be free of foreign control or influence.

British Occupation

During the British occupation of Egypt, many upper government and army posts were given to British citizens. Growing resentment of these practices was evident in the rise of newspapers, political parties, and workers' unions that espoused a nationalist viewpoint.

When World War I (1914–1918) broke out, the Ottoman Empire sided with Germany. Because Britain and the other Allied countries were fighting against Germany, Britain ended all its dealings with the Ottoman government and declared Egypt a *protectorate*. Resentment built against the British during the war as Egyptians were forced to serve in the British army and sell their cotton and livestock to the British at below-market prices.

This resentment surfaced in 1919 when the British refused to listen to the Wafd, a delegation of four nationalist leaders who demanded independence. Instead, the British government exiled the Wafd, sparking violent protests and rebellion throughout Egypt. Women in veils held demonstrations of their own, the first time upper-class women had publicly voiced their opinion on political issues.

The unrest continued for three years until Britain finally agreed to grant a provisional independence to Egypt. Although Egypt technically became an independent nation in 1922, Britain retained the right to intervene anytime it felt that its interests were in danger. Ahmad Fuad became King Fuad I (foo-AHD), the first king of Egypt.

Struggle for Full Independence

Within a year, Egypt had established a constitutional monarchy. The first parliamentary elections resulted in a victory for the Wafd. King Fuad felt that the Wafd was a threat to his power and refused to let it take office. In 1930, the king approved a revision to the constitution granting more power to himself.

Cavalrymen from the Egyptian army rehearse for a ceremony celebrating the crowning of King Farouk I. Farouk I became king in 1936 after the death of his father, King Fuad I, the first king of Egypt.

King Fuad died in 1936 and was succeeded by his son Farouk I (feh-ROOK). The original constitution was reinstated, resulting in the election once more of the Wafd to parliament. The Wafd supported the British during World War II (1939–1945). As a result, popular support shifted to other organizations and political parties, including the Muslim Brotherhood and Young Egypt, two popular paramilitary groups that pushed for societal and governmental reform through the application of Islamic principles.

Renewed calls for complete independence and the removal of British troops came after World War II. Britain refused to negotiate further and left its troops in place. Once more, rioting and demonstrations broke out in urban areas as Egyptians protested the decision.

Emotions turned against Britain even more following the creation of the Jewish state of Israel in 1948. Most Egyptians felt that Britain had facilitated the settlement of Jews in Palestine, an Arab homeland. Egypt joined other Arab nations in declaring war on Israel. The newly created Israeli state won the war and established control over much of Palestine. Of the remaining parts of Palestine, the Old City of Jerusalem and the West Bank were taken and annexed by Jordan. The Gaza Strip was taken by Egypt and put under military administration.

One of the Egyptian officers fighting against Israel was Colonel Gamal Abdel Nasser (guh-MAHL AHB-duhl NAH-ser). Dismayed by the poor performance of the Egyptian army, Nasser organized a secret group within the Egyptian army called the Free Officers. In 1952, following widespread rioting and rebellion against the British troops still in Egypt, the Free Officers overthrew King Farouk's government.

The Free Officers named General Muhammad Naguib head of the new government. Large land holdings were broken up and distributed among the *fellahin* (fel-uh-HEEN), or peasants. Political parties were banned, and, in 1953, the Free Officers declared Egypt a *republic* with Naguib as president.

Nasser's Egypt

Nasser took over as president of Egypt in 1954, after Naguib was forced from office for supporting the militant Muslim Brotherhood. Soon after that, Nasser was able to negotiate an agreement for the British to withdraw all troops, including those near the Suez Canal, by 1956. One of the most ambitious projects proposed by Nasser was the construction of the Aswan High Dam. The dam would increase the amount of land under cultivation as well as generate electricity. After the United States and Britain withdrew offers to fund the project, Nasser authorized the government's takeover of the Suez Canal. He also negotiated with the Soviet Union to provide funding for the High Dam.

The nationalization of the Suez Canal enraged the British, who deemed it vital to their economic interests in the region, and the French, who had built and operated the canal. The two countries joined together with Israel to launch an attack against Egypt. Israel took control of the Gaza Strip and the Sinai Peninsula, while Britain and France invaded the canal zone. The United Nations negotiated a cease-fire a week later, and Britain, France, and Israel were required to withdraw from Egypt's territory.

In 1958, Syria's government approached Nasser and proposed the creation of a United Arab Republic (UAR). Nasser agreed to the federation, but as Egypt began to implement socialist policies in the early 1960s, Syria withdrew from the UAR. A similar alliance with Yemen, the United Arab States, also failed.

Despite these setbacks, Nasser organized meetings of the Arab states in 1964 to address the threat by Israel to use the Jordan River for irrigation projects. During these meetings, the Palestine Liberation

GAMAL ABDEL NASSER

The first president of Egypt—Gamal Abdel Nasser—was born in Alexandria, Egypt, in 1918. His family was poor, which made it difficult for Nasser to continue his education beyond secondary school. He persevered, applying to the Royal Military Academy three times before he was admitted.

In 1948, angry at British support for the creation of a Jewish state in the Arab land of Palestine and at what they saw as an ineffective king, Nasser and other military leaders formed the Free Officers group.

Their goal was to force the British from Egypt and to replace the king with an elected president. In 1952, they launched a successful coup against King Farouk.

By 1954, Nasser was in control of the government and, two years later, became Egypt's first elected president. The British had withdrawn from Egypt, and Nasser was set to launch the first of his many reforms. His willingness to stand up to world powers such as Britain and the United States won him great admiration from the Arab world. Within Egypt, however, he was respected for his dedication to social reforms and his commitment to shoring up Egypt's economy through industrialization.

Organization (PLO) was founded as a means of controlling the actions of the Palestinian *guerrillas* (nonmilitary fighters) in Israel.

Hostilities between Israel and the Arab states increased during the mid-1960s. Israel threatened to invade Syria if guerrilla attacks across their shared border weren't stopped. In May 1967, the Soviets spread false reports that Israel was planning to attack Syria. Since Egypt and Syria had an agreement to defend each other's borders, Nasser sent

ASWAN HIGH DAM

The Aswan High Dam, located south of the city of Aswan, is considered one of the modern wonders of the world by many engineers. When the United States and Britain would not loan Egypt the money to build the dam, Egypt's president Gamal Nasser took over control of the Suez Canal. The revenues from the canal were used to pay for the construction of the dam. Technical assistance, as well as the machinery needed to build the rockfill dam, was provided by the Soviet Union.

The construction of the dam, which is 364 feet (111 meters) high, required much planning. Tens of thousands of Nubians had to be relocated to new communities, since their ancient villages would be flooded once the dam was built. In addition, the Nile Valley south of the proposed dam site was rich with archaeological treasures. The Egyptian government requested help from the international community in excavating and cataloguing as many artifacts as possible before the region was flooded. The biggest archaeological effort was the relocation of the ancient temples built by Ramses II at Abu Simbel. The two magnificent temples—one in honor of Ramses himself and the other in honor of his wife Nefertari and the goddess Hathor—were taken apart stone by stone, then rebuilt on a higher site.

The High Dam was completed in 1970 after eighteen years under construction. It cost approximately US$1 billion to build. The reservoir it created, Lake Nasser, stretches nearly 311 miles (500 kilometers) south of the dam, crossing the southern border of Egypt into Sudan. Today, the hydroelectric plants at the Aswan High Dam generate about one-fourth of Egypt's electricity.

While the dam has created environmental problems, including increased water pollution downstream from Aswan, the advantages it provides seem to outweigh the problems. With a dependable water source, farmers are able to grow more crops and increase their income levels. The drought that scorched Africa during the 1980s had little effect on Egypt, due to the vast water reserves in Lake Nasser. Likewise, the High Dam kept potentially deadly floods at bay during the 1990s.

The Aswan High Dam, here under construction in the 1960s, is located about 4 miles (6.4 kilometers) upstream from the Aswan Dam, a much smaller dam completed in 1902.

Egyptian troops to the Egyptian-Israeli border in hopes of deterring an Israeli attack on Syria. At the same time, he made clear his intention to close Israel's only access to the Red Sea.

On June 5, the Jordanian army began to bombard Jerusalem, ignoring Israeli assurances that Israel had no interest in a war with

Israeli soldiers dance in celebration at the Western Wall, a sacred religious site in the old city of Jerusalem, during the Six-Day War of 1967. They were the first Israelis to see the wall since that section of the city went under Arab control in the late 1940s. Egypt lost many soldiers and most of its military equipment in the war.

Jordan. In response, Israel invaded East Jerusalem and the West Bank and launched attacks on Egypt and Syria. The strikes in Egypt happened so quickly that many of Egypt's military planes were destroyed before the pilots could reach them. Within three days, the Israeli army had reached the Suez Canal. By the time the Arab states and Israel reached a cease-fire agreement on June 11, Israel was in control of all of historical Palestine, as well as Egypt's Sinai Peninsula and the Golan Heights in Syria.

In what became known as the Six-Day War, over 11,500 Egyptian soldiers were killed. Nearly half that many had been captured by the Israelis. And about 80 percent of Egypt's military equipment was destroyed. Nasser apologized to the Egyptian people for his part in the debacle and resigned. The people refused to accept his resignation, however, and Nasser remained president of Egypt.

Fighting between the Israelis and Egyptians continued until August 1970, when Israel, Egypt, and Jordan signed a cease-fire agreement. When PLO leader Yasir Arafat criticized Egypt's actions and attacked Jordan, Nasser cut off Egyptian funding to the organization. In September, Nasser negotiated a cease-fire between the PLO and Jordan. The stress of the meeting took its toll, however; Nasser died of a heart attack soon after.

A New President

Following Nasser's death, his vice president—Anwar Sadat (AHN-war sah-DAHT)—assumed the presidency. He moved quickly to revise the constitution. When the Soviet Union refused to sell weapons to Egypt, Sadat ordered all Soviet advisers to leave the country. Although Sadat had hoped this measure would improve relations with the United States, nothing changed.

In 1973, Egypt and Syria secretly agreed to attack Israeli forces stationed in the Sinai and Golan Heights— lands that they had controlled until 1967. The element of surprise resulted in the recapture of some of their respective territories, but Israel soon regained control of the regions and advanced even further toward Cairo and Damascus. The fighting continued until the Soviet Union threatened to intervene and the United States put its troops on nuclear alert. By 1974, the U.S. secretary of state, Henry Kissinger, was able to negotiate an

The Arab-Israeli War of 1973 is also known as the Yom Kippur War or the Ramadan War because it was launched during these holy days.

agreement between Israel and Syria calling for the Israelis to withdraw from the Golan Heights region. A similar agreement was signed by Israel and Egypt in 1975.

Following Kissinger's negotiations, the relationship between Egypt and the United States warmed. Further peace talks between Egypt and Israel were held at Camp David, the U.S. presidential retreat in Maryland, in 1978. The Camp David Accords, as the agreements became known, were the basis for a peace treaty signed in 1979.

Although Sadat was awarded the 1978 Nobel Peace Prize for his leadership in the Camp David Accords, he was shunned by the Arab community. An economic boycott by Arab nations hurt Egypt's economy. Many Islamic and socialist leaders were arrested for undermining Sadat's authority. On October 6, 1981, a group of Islamist military officers retaliated by assassinating Sadat.

Egypt Today

Sadat's vice president, Hosni Mubarak (HOHS-nee moo-BAH-rahk), ascended to the presidency following Sadat's assassination. His major goal during his first years as president was to restore relations with the Arab community. By 1987, Egypt had reestablished diplomatic relations with most Arab countries.

In 1990, following Iraq's invasion of Kuwait, Mubarak supported the alliance led by the United States that forced Saddam Hussein's troops back to Iraq. However, fundamentalist Islamic groups in Egypt opposed the Western presence in the Persian Gulf. Many attempts were made to overthrow Mubarak's government, including an assassination attempt in 1995. Attacks on Copts, Western tourists, and politicians who didn't support a strong Islamic position became more frequent in the late 1990s, a sign of discontent with the status quo. In response, the government cracked down on Islamic and other opposition groups.

In 2003, as the United States and its coalition forces prepared to invade Iraq to force Saddam Hussein from power, Mubarak placed the blame for the conflict on Hussein. Many Egyptians, shocked that Mubarak didn't chastise the United States for its aggressiveness in pursuing Hussein, began publicly criticizing Mubarak. In early April, as the Iraqi capital of Baghdad fell, Mubarak took the lead in voicing Arab support for an Iraqi transitional government.

Economy

Throughout the 1990s, Egypt worked with International Monetary Fund advisers to improve economic policies. Inflation was controlled and foreign investment increased. Since 2000, however, the economy has slowed.

Business and Industry

Agriculture, especially the cultivation of long-staple cotton, has long been the cornerstone of Egypt's economy. In modern times, however, there has been a push to diversify the economy. As a result, the petroleum industry and tourism have joined agriculture as leading contributors to the Egyptian economy. Much of the cash coming into Egypt comes from *remittances,* or money sent to family members by Egyptians who work in other countries.

In the 1990s, Egypt improved its economy, although the economy slowed somewhat at the beginning of the twenty-first century. This picture shows the small but busy stock exchange in Cairo.

Agriculture

Following the construction of the Aswan High Dam, the amount of land available to cultivate in Egypt increased dramatically. Because farmers have a dependable source of water year-round, they are able to grow two or three crops rather than one. Egyptian cotton, prized for its long fibers and softness, is grown as a cash crop. Wheat, corn, and rice are also widely grown. In addition to the crops grown for export, many farmers grow fruits and vegetables to sell or trade at local markets.

Petroleum

Egypt was the first Middle Eastern country to discover oil. Today, petroleum production and refining make a major contribution to the economy. Enough oil is produced from wells in the Gulf of Suez, the Western and Eastern Deserts, and the Sinai Peninsula to provide most of Egypt's energy. In addition, about 40 percent of Egypt's export revenues come from the sale of petroleum and petroleum products. In recent years, the discovery of large natural gas reserves has created a

Workers handle cotton at a mill in Tanta, Egypt. For thousands of years many people have considered Egyptian cotton to be the world's finest. Cotton is second only to oil in Egyptian exports and, including the textiles made from it, earns roughly $500 million per year.

great deal of excitement. Economists expect that Egypt will be able to develop a strong market for gas exports.

Tourism

Since its earliest days, people from other countries have wanted to visit Egypt. Its vibrant cities, ancient pyramids, and desert oases have lured many explorers over the millennia.

Today, tourism is a major source of Egypt's income. Most visitors are eager to visit the great pyramids and temples of ancient Egypt and learn more about the splendor of that age. Some want to travel from oasis to oasis, sampling the flavor of a traditional way of life that is thousands of years old. The coastal cities draw visitors who want to play on the beach and enjoy great snorkeling and scuba diving, while trips down the Nile in traditional *feluccas* (sailboats) introduce tourists to the great cities of ancient Egypt.

Following terrorist attacks on the United States in 2001, Egypt's tourist industry slowed. It was further harmed by tensions between the United States and Iraq, which culminated in war in Iraq in 2003.

Media and Communications

Cairo has a long history as an important center of Islamic learning. This, combined with Egypt's reputation as a leader in Middle Eastern politics, has given Egyptian newspapers a wide audience in the Arab world. The government restricts free speech on many issues, however, since Sadat's assassination in 1981 by Islamic extremists. The government can arrest journalists who criticize its policies or actions too harshly. As a result, journalists generally censor themselves when commenting on the president's actions.

Television is very popular in Egypt. Since 1995, most Arab-language television shows and movies have been produced in Egypt. In 1998, the government established NileSat, Egyptian satellite television. In its early days, it hosted thirty channels. Today, 160 television channels are offered. These include Egyptian and Arab stations as well as international channels such as CNN and Showtime. In addition, 135 radio stations are offered through satellite. The government expects that high-speed Internet services will be offered through NileSat in the near future.

> *Did You Know?*
>
> Because of the prevalence of Egyptian films, the Egyptian dialect of the Arabic language is widely familiar in the Arab world.

Basic telephone service—controlled by the government—was upgraded in the 1990s. Cellular telephones are becoming more popular. Foreign countries offer most cellular services.

Religion and Beliefs

The ancient Egyptians worshiped many gods. They believed that the pharaohs were descendants of Horus, the god of light. When other civilizations conquered and ruled Egypt, foreign gods were introduced. In the first century c.e., Christianity was introduced. By the sixth century, most Egyptians had accepted the idea of one god and converted to Christianity. These Christians were called Copts, after the Greek word for "Egyptian." In the seventh century, Arab invaders brought the religion of Islam to Egypt. After years of persecution by the Byzantine Church, many Coptic Christians eagerly converted to Islam. Today, about 94 percent of the population follows Islam. While most of the

Coptic Christians celebrate a Christmas mass in Cairo. Due to differences between the familiar Gregorian calendar and that used by Coptic Christians, Christmas is celebrated on January 7 in Egypt. Although Coptic Christians are a small minority of the population, Christmas was made a national holiday in Egypt in 2003.

remaining Egyptians are Coptic Christians, some still follow traditional religions.

As in other predominantly Islamic countries, religious considerations are evident in every aspect of Egyptian life. Every day in cities and towns, the *muezzin* (moo-EHZ-zin), a Muslim crier, calls people to prayer. Pork and alcohol, items forbidden by the Qur'an, are rarely available. The official language is Arabic, the language of the Qur'an. The work and school week begins on Saturday or Sunday and ends on Thursday, with time off on Friday—the Islamic holy day.

Islamic Beliefs

Muslims follow the teachings of the Prophet Mohammad, who established Islam in the seventh century. They believe in one God—Allah—who revealed the Qur'an to Mohammad, the last in a series of prophets that includes Abraham and Jesus. Devout Muslims observe the five pillars of Islam: professing that "there is no God but God and Mohammad is his messenger," praying five times daily, fasting during the holy month of Ramadan, giving alms (charity) to the poor, and making a pilgrimage to Mecca, the birthplace of Mohammad. (To learn more about Islam, see page ix in the introduction to this volume.)

Coptic Beliefs

The Coptic Church was established in Egypt by Saint Mark, one of the disciples of Jesus Christ. It played a major role in the development of the organized Christian church, defining doctrine (religious beliefs) and practices. Copts have the same belief in God as the Father, the Son, and the Holy Spirit as other Christians. They believe that Jesus Christ is the son of God and that through faith in Christ, people can be saved from their sins.

Copts celebrate seven major holy feasts: Annunciation, Christmas, Theophany (or the appearance of their god in human form), Palm Sunday, Easter, Ascension, and the Pentecost. Of these, Easter is the holiest day, followed by Christmas. The Coptic Church uses the older Julian calendar, which is shorter than the Gregorian calendar that is widely used today. As a result, Copts celebrate their holy days on different dates than most other Christians. For example, Christmas is celebrated on January 7.

Copts believe in fasting during each holy season. Each year, devout Copts fast on more than 200 days. (Those who are ill or have special circumstances are generally excused from fasting.) During a fast, no food or drink can be consumed between sunrise and sunset. Meals prepared during fasting seasons must contain no animal products, including milk and butter.

Coptic Christians have been persecuted by other groups, from the Byzantine Christian Church in the fifth and sixth centuries to the Islamic extremists of today, ever since the Coptic Church was established. (For more information about Christianity, please see page ix in the introduction to this volume.)

Everyday Life

Because Egypt has such a hot climate, most daily activities take place in the mornings and evenings. In the early afternoon, when temperatures

Many people, including this family in Cairo, find that motorcycles, although they don't look safe, are the fastest, cheapest way to get around the crowded, bustling city.

are the highest, the pace slows. Businesses and schools close. Families gather in their homes to rest and relax for a few hours. Then businesses reopen and the hustle and bustle begin again.

Family Life

Family is the center of Egyptian life today, just as it has been for thousands of years. The extended family—grandparents, aunts, uncles, and cousins—gather together often, whether for festive celebrations following Ramadan or for simple picnics after religious services.

In traditional families, the women rarely venture from their homes. They prepare the meals and care for their children, but the men make the major decisions for the family. Muslim men are allowed to have up to four wives, provided that they can support each of them equally. In reality, few men take more than one wife.

Husbands and wives have more equal roles within modern families, although men still typically have the final word on any major decision. Women often work outside the home. In recent years, as educational opportunities have opened up for women, some have found work in professions such as medicine, law, and science.

Despite these gains, women do not enjoy the same rights as men in many instances. Although Egyptian women are guaranteed financial independence with control over some legal matters—as witnesses in court or in matters of inheritance, the laws still favor men.

Young children are treasured and pampered, whether they grow up in traditional or modern families. Large families were the norm in the past, especially in rural areas, since more children meant more help with the family's work. In recent years, however, as Egypt has become more industrialized, couples are having fewer children. All parents, even those who still follow a traditional nomadic lifestyle, realize the importance of education for today's children.

Traditionally, children live with their parents until they are married. However, as more young people continue their education through the university level, many are moving away from home to find work. Some relocate within Egypt, but a growing number are moving out of the country. While arranged marriages are a tradition, more and more parents are giving their children the final decision on whether to marry the person chosen for them.

Dress

Clothing styles vary dramatically in Egypt. Traditional clothing is still worn by many Egyptians, both in the city and in rural areas. Men who dress in the traditional style wear white cotton pants topped with a tunic called a *galabia* (guh-LAH-bee-uh). A small skullcap or turban covers the head. In the urban business districts, Western-style suits are very common.

Women often wear brightly colored clothing in their homes. Those who are more traditional don a cloak called a *melaya* when they appear in public. In urban areas, many women wear Western-style dresses. However, the dresses nearly always have long sleeves; it is considered immodest to appear with one's arms uncovered in public. For the same reasons of modesty, women wearing nontraditional clothing often cover their hair with a scarf.

Clothing in Egypt ranges from the traditional to the modern, which often imitates familiar Western styles of dress. This woman and two girls are covered in traditional cloaks as they pass another woman in less traditional clothing.

Women receive a dowry of gold and silver jewelry from their husbands when they get married. Traditionally, women wear the jewelry at all times—necklaces, bracelets, anklets, and rings. If their husbands should happen to divorce them without warning, the dowry provides a source of income.

Education

Traditionally, the only schools in Egypt were Qur'anic schools where boys learned to chant the Qur'an. As the nineteenth century began, the government worked with local communities to establish modern secular schools.

Nasser's government made education of all children a priority. Beginning in the early 1950s, schools were built and teachers were trained. Free primary education is available to all Egyptian children. Those who can pass the tests required for admission to preparatory schools, secondary schools, and universities can also attend free of charge. Most children attend primary school, and an increasing number of young people from both rural and urban areas are continuing on to

THE EGYPTIAN SCHOOL SYSTEM

If you were a student in an Egyptian school, your day would start early. Schools often begin classes at 7:00 A.M. to take advantage of the coolest part of the day.

Primary Schools

A typical primary school classroom serves thirty-four students, ages six through twelve. Reading, writing, and math are taught during the first two years. Science and religious studies are added during the third year. A foreign language, usually English, is introduced the following year. Learning a non-Arabic language can be challenging. Not only do students have to learn new words, they also have to learn a new alphabet system and they have to read and write in a different direction (from left to right rather than right to left). Since primary school is the only formal education some children receive, it often includes practical subjects such as sewing and cooking for the girls and agricultural practices or metalworking for the boys.

Postprimary Levels

Students who wish to continue their education past primary school must pass an exam. Preparatory schools, similar to junior high schools in the United States, offer three years of academic study. Students who pass the exam after completing preparatory school are invited to attend secondary school. There are two types of secondary schools. The first offers an academic program that prepares students for university studies. The second is a technical school, providing practical career training in agriculture, business, and industry. Students who attend universities often study for careers in medicine, law, or education.

college. Poverty and rapid population growth, however, have set limits on access and attendance.

Recreation and Leisure

The Egyptian culture is very social. People enjoy taking walks and visiting friends and family at the end of the day. In the cities, street performers entertain the crowds each evening. Men often congregate in coffeehouses to discuss current news and play games such as dominoes or backgammon. Attending the most recent movie with friends is also a favorite pastime.

As Egypt becomes more industrialized and income levels rise, people are finding more time for leisure. Sporting events such as soccer—called football in Egypt—attract enthusiastic players and fans. Clubs have sprung up to encourage specific sports and activities such as tennis, rowing, and scuba diving. Some popular recreational activities, such as fishing, were necessary for survival not so very long ago.

Egyptian children enjoy many of the same games as American children. Hide-and-go-seek and tag are among the games played by neighborhood friends or at family picnics.

A bread vendor in Cairo carries his wares on his head. In rural areas of Egypt, bread is more than something to eat with dinner: people often use it in place of a fork to scoop up food.

Food

The social nature of Egyptian life is readily apparent in the warm hospitality offered to guests. As in other Arab countries, the gracious and generous treatment of guests is of prime importance. Food and drink are always offered. Guests are expected to accept the lavish offerings; to refuse to partake is very rude. In fact, if guests don't leave the table feeling quite stuffed, Egyptians feel that they have failed as hosts.

KOSHARI (RICE, LENTILS, AND VERMICELLI)

Traditionally, the lentils, rice, and pasta are cooked separately and layered in a serving dish. This recipe simplifies the process.

Sauce:
3 tablespoons extra-virgin olive oil
1/2 cup very finely chopped onion
4 cloves garlic, crushed
1 14-ounce can peeled tomatoes, coarsely chopped
1/4 teaspoon finely ground black pepper
1/4 teaspoon crushed red pepper flakes, or to taste

Koshari:
8 tablespoons extra-virgin olive oil
1-1/2 cups sliced onions
1/2 cup vermicelli broken into 1-inch pieces
1-1/4 cups brown lentils
1-1/4 cups basmati rice
Salt

Combine the olive oil and chopped onions for the sauce in a saucepan and sauté over medium heat until the onions are golden. Add the garlic and stir for a few more minutes, then add the tomatoes and spices. Increase the heat to medium-high and cook for 10 to 20 minutes, or until thickened. Use a food mill or processor to puree the sauce mixture. Keep the sauce warm while preparing the koshari.

To make the koshari, heat the oil over medium heat. Add the onions and sauté, stirring occasionally, until they are golden brown and caramelized. Remove the onions with a slotted spoon, and place them on paper towels to drain the oil. Add the vermicelli to the oil in the pan and sauté until browned. Set aside.

Put the lentils in a saucepan with 5 cups of water. Bring to a boil, then reduce the heat and simmer, covered, for 15 to 30 minutes, until quite tender.

Rinse the rice under cold water and add to the lentils when they are tender. Simmer for 10 minutes, then stir in the vermicelli and oil from the pan. Add salt to taste. Wrap the lid of the pan with a clean kitchen towel, place the lid back on the pan, and remove the pan from the heat. Let sit for 10 minutes, or until the vermicelli is tender and the liquid is fully absorbed. Stir in half the caramelized onions, reserving the other half for garnish. (Use a fork to stir the rice so you can fluff it up at the same time.)

Transfer the koshari to a serving dish and ladle the tomato sauce all over. Scatter the remaining caramelized onions on top. Serve hot or at room temperature.

Serves 8.

Source: *Mediterranean Street Food* by Anissa Helou.

A typical meal for guests begins with an often vast assortment of appetizers. These savory dishes may include vegetables and dips as well as elaborate salads. After the appetizers, the main meal is served. If at all possible, meat will be served when guests are present, even if it presents a financial hardship for the family. The meat or poultry dish is accompanied by bread, rice, and vegetables. Diners in rural areas often use pieces of bread to scoop up their main dish rather than forks. The right hand is always used for eating; the left is considered dirty. Desserts are generally sweet and use readily available ingredients such as dates and other fruits. The meal ends with coffee or tea. Guests are expected to leave a little food on their plates at the end of the meal to show appreciation for hosts who provided such an abundant feast that it couldn't all be eaten.

While entertaining guests requires elaborate preparation, meals eaten at home with the family are a simpler affair. Egyptians often have bread and fava beans for breakfast, along with strong coffee. The main meal is served at midday when the family gathers at home. This meal often includes a few appetizers, a main dish, fresh bread, and fruit for dessert. Because meat is expensive and spoils quickly in the heat, vegetarian main dishes are common in Egypt. Religious restrictions, such as the fasting seasons of the Coptic Church, have also contributed to the development of many flavorful vegetarian dishes. The evening meal is typically light, perhaps a few appetizers or a snack such as falafel—a treat made by stuffing a fried, spicy chickpea mixture into pita bread and topping it with fresh or pickled vegetables.

In large towns and cities, vendors sell street food—falafel, barbecued meat, pastries, and other treats. Egyptians enjoy these light meals or snacks throughout the day.

Holidays and Festivals

Holidays present opportunities for family members to gather for solemn religious observations as well as lively celebrations. Many of these holidays are religious, but Egyptians also celebrate the arrival of spring and patriotic holidays.

Religious Celebrations

Islamic holidays are widely celebrated, since over 90 percent of Egyptians are Muslim. The most important of these holidays is the month of Ramadan. Muslims fast between sunrise and sunset during this month. Their hunger and thirst are intended to build compassion for the less fortunate who are hungry every day. Prayer and meditation are especially important during this month, as individuals focus on their relationship with Allah. Families break the fast each day after sundown with a filling meal known as *iftar* (if-TAR).

Did You Know?

Many houses in rural Egypt are decorated with pictures that illustrate the owner's pilgrimage to Mecca. They are known as hajj houses.

At the end of Ramadan comes Eid al-Fitr, a joyous holiday that lasts three days. Families and friends celebrate with new clothes, gifts, visiting, and lavish feasts.

Egyptians also celebrate Eid al-Adha, the Feast of the Sacrifice. This holiday takes place at the end of the hajj (pilgrimage to Mecca) season. Families sacrifice an animal such as a goat and share the meat with the poor.

Worshipers gather for prayers on the first day of Ramadan, Islam's holy month, at a mosque in Cairo. Muslims fast each day of this month, breaking their fast in the evenings with a filling meal, which will sustain them until the next evening.

Egyptians often commemorate the Prophet Mohammad's birthday with carnivals. Children and adults alike enjoy carnival rides and the festive atmosphere.

The most important holiday season in the Coptic Church is the Feast of the Resurrection, or Easter. The Coptic observance begins fifty-five days before Easter. During this time, Christians do not eat or drink between midnight and 3 P.M., the hour, according to tradition, that Jesus died on the cross. When they do break the Easter season's fast, the Copts eat only vegetarian dishes. This fast honors Lent, the forty days Jesus spent fasting in the wilderness before his crucifixion when he was tempted by Satan, and includes Holy Week (the week prior to Easter) and a week of preparation before Lent.

On Easter Sunday, families attend a church service that may include a dramatization of the crucifixion and resurrection. A feast is prepared, with dishes that were forbidden during the Easter fast. Colored eggs and salted fish—symbols of Jesus and new life—are also part of the celebratory feast.

Did You Know?

Copts enjoy a sweet bread called *kahk* during the Christmas season. Muslims enjoy the same treat during Eid al-Fitr.

Coptic Christian pope Shenouda III (center) blesses the bread during a midnight Christmas mass in 1996.

Christmas, which commemorates the birth of Christ, is another important holy day in the Coptic Church. Because the Coptic Church's calendar is based on the older Julian calendar, Christmas is celebrated on January 7 rather than December 25. Because Jesus, Mary, and Joseph had to flee to Egypt to find safety soon after Jesus' birth, Christmas is celebrated with special pleasure in Egypt.

Devout Copts fast throughout Advent, which lasts from November 25 through January 6. However, most Coptic Christians only fast during the week leading up to Christmas. Special concerts of Christmas music are held during this season. A special church service, the Nativity mass, is held at midnight on January 6. After the service, families celebrate with a feast. Children receive gifts and new clothes at this time. Just as in the West, Egyptian Christians decorate Christmas trees with ornaments and lights. However, the trees are often artificial.

Other Celebrations

Sham el-Nasseem, "The Scent of the Spring Breeze," is observed on the Monday following the Coptic Easter. Many families enjoy this thousand-year-old celebration of spring with picnics on the banks of the Nile. Egyptian patriotic holidays include Revolution Day (July 23), which commemorates the 1952 revolution and the creation of the republic, and Armed Forces Day (October 6), which marks the surprise attack on Israel in 1973 as Egypt battled to win back control of the Sinai Peninsula.

The Arts

Egypt has a long history of creative arts, from architecture and textiles to literature and film. While traditional crafts continue to be practiced, Egyptians today exercise their creativity in other areas as well.

Visual Arts

Ancient Egyptians were known for their artwork—fine sculptures, intricate wood carvings, and detailed paintings. These items, along with gold jewelry, filled the tombs of pharaohs and queens. After the Arab conquest in the seventh century, Islamic art styles flourished. These included arabesque—designs made from elaborate geometric patterns—

and Arabic calligraphy—the art of writing excerpts from the Qur'an as decoration. Textile crafts, while practical, were also highly decorative.

Today, traditional craftspeople sell their wares in *souks,* or markets, throughout Egypt. From richly detailed rugs and finely embroidered cotton cloth to gold and silver jewelry and items decorated with ancient Egyptian *hieroglyphics* (writing with pictures or symbols), traditional crafts with a modern flair are proudly offered to passersby.

Egyptian visual artists are painters and sculptors. They carry on the traditions of their ancient forebears, although many have adopted other styles. Some, like Mohammed Nagui (1888–1956), studied painting under Western teachers when Egypt was occupied by Britain. His impressionist-style paintings of his native land are displayed in several of Egypt's museums. Today, Nagui is known as the founder of modern Egyptian painting.

Theater and Film

Egyptians were introduced to theater in the nineteenth century, when contact with the French and British increased. From that point on,

Egyptian actor Omar Sharif stands at left in a scene from the 1962 film Lawrence of Arabia. *The movie, which also starred Anthony Quinn (right) and Peter O'Toole (center) in the title role, won the Academy Award for Best Picture that year.*

Egyptians made this art form their own. One of the earliest playwrights was Ya'qub Sanu'a (1839–1912), who wrote theatrical plays that poked fun at the upper class and Egypt's leaders. Playwrights such as Tawfiq al-Hakim later used the theater to explore dramatic themes, including the influence of Western cultures on Egypt's Arab culture.

In the 1930s, the Egyptian film industry was established. Egypt has since evolved into the center of film and television production for Arab countries. One of the best-known Egyptian actors in the West is Omar Sharif. After finding fame as an actor in Egypt, Sharif starred in the English-language films *Lawrence of Arabia* and *Doctor Zhivago*. In 1968, after he starred with Barbra Streisand in *Funny Girl*—in which Sharif's character has an affair with a Jewish girl—Sharif's films were banned in Egypt.

Conservative religious scholars have long argued that the theater is forbidden by Islam, equating its fictional characters with "intentional lies." Objections were also made on the grounds that women should not publicly display their bodies. The same arguments were used later against the film industry. Despite this opposition, Egyptians as a whole have embraced the theater and film industries.

THE STAR OF THE EAST

One of Egypt's favorite singers was Umm Kulthum (1904–1975). (Her name is also seen as Omm or Oum Kolthum.) Known as "The Star of the East," Umm Kulthum was born in a small village in the Nile Delta. Her father, a village religious leader, often performed the music for religious ceremonies and weddings. As a child, Kulthum's voice was so strong that her father often invited her to sing with him during performances to earn additional money for the family. However, she had to dress as a boy in order to perform in the ceremonies.

At nineteen, Kulthum and her family moved to Cairo. She quickly gained a following and soon was awarded a recording contract. Kulthum became even more famous in the 1930s and 1940s when she appeared in motion picture musicals. Although she started her career singing traditional Arabic music, Kulthum adopted popular music in the 1960s. As her popularity grew, she became more outspoken on political issues.

In a career that spanned fifty years, Umm Kulthum recorded more than 300 songs. Although she died in 1975, her songs are still popular throughout the Arab world.

Music and Dance

Music and dancing are integral to Egyptian celebrations. Egyptians enjoy many types of music, from traditional Arab music to folk music from rural areas to Western pop and country-western music. In recent years, popular musicians have combined elements of the different styles to produce songs with traditional lyrics or melodies that are set to a pop or country rhythm.

Traditional folk dances, once used in religious ceremonies, are enjoying a renaissance after years of being overshadowed by more modern dances. One traditional dance style, known in the West as belly dancing, is performed in many settings, from family parties to nightclubs. Discos in the larger towns and cities attract many young people who enjoy Western-style dances, while family get-togethers or celebrations often include traditional Arabic dances.

Literature

Egypt was among the first civilizations to develop a writing system. The system used a combination of pictures and symbols called *hieroglyphs* that were written on paper made from papyrus reed or carved into the walls of the pyramids and temples. Ancient Egyptians use hieroglyphs to record heroic deeds and business transactions. As Arab culture spread through Egypt, the art of poetry thrived as well. Writers created verses extolling love's tragedies and triumphs, victories and defeats in battle, and delight in everyday life. Poetry is still revered in Egypt, but over the last hundred years, writers have begun exploring other forms of writing as well, including novels, short stories, and plays.

Naguib Mahfouz, one of Egypt's most famous writers, was awarded the Nobel Prize for Literature in 1988. He was the first Arab writer to receive the Nobel Prize. Mahfouz wrote more than forty novels and short story collections, as well as thirty screenplays for movies. His stories paint a picture of Egyptian life, usually from the viewpoint of the poorest people in the city.

GLOSSARY

annex to take control of another country's territory; one country may annex another by agreement or through the use of force

caliph an Islamic spiritual leader, the successor to the Prophet Mohammad

caliphate Islamic realm, ruled by a religious and political leader called a caliph

coup shortened version of *coup d'état*, the overthrow of a government, usually by a small group

dynasty a family of powerful leaders that is maintained over generations

enosis union; used to describe the move to make Cyprus part of Greece

exile to force people to leave their homeland for political or religious reasons; a person who is forced to leave his or her country

guerrilla describes aggressive, unconventional attacks by armed fighters, usually those who are trying to overthrow their government; one of the armed fighters

nationalist a person who supports nationalism, the belief that one's country should be independent

partition the division of a country into separate political units

protectorate a relationship in which a strong country agrees to protect a smaller country or region in return for some degree of control over the smaller country's affairs

republic a government whose leader is not a monarch; generally the leader is a president who is elected by citizens of the country

BIBLIOGRAPHY

About.com. "The Aswan High Dam." 1/26/98. <http://geography. about.com/library/weekly/aa012698.htm>

Adherents.com. "Major Religions of the World Ranked by Number of Adherents." 9/6/02. <http://www.adherents.com/Religions_ By_Adherents.html>

Aeolos. "Destination Cyprus." <http://www.aeolos.com/ main/main.asp?gid=197>

American Chamber of Commerce in Egypt. "The Egyptian Petroleum Industry." <http://www.amcham.org.eg/BSAC/ StudiesSeries/Report33.asp>

Arabic News.com. "Exploring Aspects of Modern Arts in Middle East." 1/23/02. <http://www.arabicnews.com/ansub/Daily/Day/ 020123/2002012339.html>

————. "Nagui's Museum, Landmark of Modern Egyptian Art." 9/24/01. <http://www.arabicnews.com/ansub/Daily/Day/ 010924/2001092436.html>

Armenians in Cyprus. <www.hayem.org>

Asante, Molefi Kete. *Culture and Customs of Egypt*. Westport, CT: Greenwood Press, 2002.

Bahrain National Museum. "Hall of Dilmun." <http://www.bnmuseum.com/dilmun.htm>

BBC News.com. "Country Profile: Egypt." 3/3/03. <http://news.bbc.co. uk/1/hi/world/middle_east/country_profiles/737642.stm>

Campbell, Kay Hardy. "Traditional Music from the Arabian Gulf." *Middle East Studies Association Bulletin.* 7/96. <http://w3fp. arizona.edu/mesassoc/Bulletin/campbell.htm>

Chapman, G.W. "Afforestation Techniques in Cyprus." Food and Agriculture Organization of the United Nations. *Unasylva* 6:4, 1952. <http://www.fao.org/docrep/x5365e/x5365e03.htm>

The Cyprus Homepage. "Folk Art and Cyprus Handicrafts." <http://kypros.org/Cyprus/Folk/pottery.html>

Cyprus Museum of Natural History. <http://www.natmuseum.org.cy/>

Cyprus Tourism Organization. <http://www.cyprustourism.org/ cyprus.html>

Delta Tours Egypt. "Egypt's Oases." <http://www.deltatoursegypt.com/ hotels/oases/egypt_oases.htm>

Department of Civil and Environmental Engineering, University of South Florida. "Modern Wonders of the World." <http://ce.eng.usf.edu/pharos/wonders/other.html>

Discover Armenia. "The Armenian Church." <http://www.armeniaemb.org/ DiscoverArmenia/ArmenianChurch/Index.htm>

Dowell, Roxanne. "Easter: A Coptic Celebration." *Middle East Times.* <http://www.metimes.com/issue98-11/commu/celeb.htm>

The European Union: A Guide for Americans. 2002 Edition. <http://www.eurunion.org/infores/euguide/euguide.htm#contents>

Ferguson, Barbara G.B. "Bahrain: A Special International Report." *Washington Times.* 2000. <http://www.internationalspecialreports. com/middleeast/00/bahrain/index.html>

Fox, Mary Virginia. *Bahrain.* Chicago: Childrens Press, 1992.

Giorgoudes, Panicos. "Music of Cyprus." Ethnomusicology Research Program, University of Cyprus. 1999. <http://www.ucy.ac.cy/research/ethno/article2.htm>

Goldstein, Joyce. *The Mediterranean Kitchen*. New York: William Morrow, 1989.

Greek Spider: Your Guide to Greece and Cyprus. <http://www.greekspider.com/greekcustoms/santaclaus.htm>

Helou, Anissa. *Mediterranean Street Food*. New York: HarperCollins, 2002.

Little Horus. <http://www.horus.ics.org.eg/html/about_little_horus.html>

Lyle, Garry. *Let's Visit Cyprus*. London: Burke, 1984.

Metz, Helen Chapin, ed. *Persian Gulf States: Country Studies*. Federal Research Division, Library of Congress, 1993. <http://memory.loc.gov/frd/cs/cshome.html>

Moeller, Susan C. "An Overview of Eastern Orthodoxy." International School of Theology. 7/13/02. <http://www.leaderu.com/isot/docs/orthdox3.html>

North Cyprus.com. <http://www.cypnet.co.uk/ncyprus/people/cypmaronites/>

Poullis, Alkis. "The Lefkara Lace Home Page." 1997. <http://www.cyculture.net/lefkara/>

Rice, Aaron. "Nubia." Adapted from the Oriental Institute Museum. 3/7/95. <http://www.byu.edu/ipt/projects/egypt/Nubia.html>

Rich, Tracey. Judaism 101. <http://www.jewfaq.org>

Salloum, Habeeb. *From the Lands of Figs and Olives*. Brooklyn: Interlink Books, 1995.

Sami, Nermin, and Jimmy Dunn. "Christmas in Egypt." TourEgypt.net. <http://www.touregypt.net/featurestories/christmas.htm>

Sengupta, Somini. "Bahrain's Women Take a Step Toward Political Power." *New York Times*. 10/24/02. <http://query.nytimes.com/ search/restricted/article?res=F20F1EF839580C778EDDA90994 DA404482>

Shaw, Elliott, ed. "Overview of World Religions." Religion and Ethics Department, St. Martins College. Lancaster, England. <http://philtar.ucsm.ac.uk/encyclopedia/index.html>

Solsten, Eric, ed. *Cyprus: A Country Study*. Federal Research Division, Library of Congress. Washington, DC: Department of the Army, 1993. <http://lcweb2.loc.gov/frd/cs/cytoc.html>

United States Agency for International Development. "Protecting Egypt's Environment." <http://www.usaid.gov/regions/ ane/newpages/perspectives/egypt/egenv.htm>

U.S. Central Intelligence Agency. *The World Factbook 2002*. <http://www.cia.gov/cia/publications/factbook/index.html>

United States Department of State. "Post Report 2001: Cyprus." <http://www.americanembassy.org.cy/postrep.htm>

Weiss-Armush, Anne Marie. *The Arabian Delights Cookbook*. Los Angeles: Lowell House, 1994.

xe.com. *"The Full Universal Currency Converter."* <http://www.xe.com/ucc/full.shtml>

Yahoo! Movie Biographies. "Omar Sharif." <http://movies.yahoo.com/ shop?d=hc&id=1800019467&cf=biog&intl=us>

CUMULATIVE INDEX

Note: Page numbers in *italics* indicate illustrations and captions.